BEING
AND
BECOMING

*A Book of Lessons in the Science of Mind
Showing How to Find the Personal Spirit*

By

FENWICKE LINDSAY HOLMES

NEW YORK
ROBERT M. McBRIDE & CO.
1925

FOREWORD.

THIS book is written to show how we know that there is a universal intelligence; how that intelligence or being becomes manifest, or the passing of spirit into form; the method by which we can control the form it shall take for us as individuals; the way in which we can harness cosmic forces; and above all it is written to make plain the personal relation of our own self with the Greater Self whose life we share.

The highest purpose of this science of thinking is to develop a conscious feeling of our oneness with Spirit. By Spirit we mean the absolute of Life, Love and Wisdom. "Thou hast made us for Thyself; and our hearts are restless 'til they rest in Thee." This, therefore, is the Book of Love and explains fully the nature of the feeling-life.

Without detracting from the essential teaching of the new science, that man is endowed with perfect freedom and can make his life what he will by his conscious choices, I have shown here how we may still keep the delightful fellowship of the Personal Spirit and the sense of a Presence that guides us in all the affairs of life.

FENWICKE LINDSAY HOLMES.

Los Angeles, Calif.
Feb. 6, 1920.

CONTENTS

PART ONE

BEING AS THE IMPERSONAL LIFE

CONTENTS

good, since Being becomes manifest either for good
or ill according to the idea or thought which forms
the mold for its expression. This truth does away
with any concept of a dual mind.

VIII. MAN'S GREATER BODY AND THE FEELING-LIFE 57

Being is not only a thinker but also a lover. While
feeling is indeed a fine form of thinking, yet we
may speak of Being as the Feeling-life. Each of
us has a well-developed feeling nature which we
derive from Original Feeling or God. This feeling-
life operates not only within the area of what we
commonly know as the physical body, but also
functions through an area of fine vibration all
about us which is so sensitive that it takes the impression even of thought forces. We are thus constantly directly in contact with others through the
very atmosphere. This is illustrated in the aura
and in the odic fluid. Through both the greater
body and the lesser, there run the finer feeling
forces which lie between man's conscious thought
and his body. The body is profoundly affected by
whatever affects the feeling-life; and as the latter
is impersonal, every thought and feeling we experience is registered directly on the body and affairs.
Thus our bodies are subject to all mental influences
that come to us; and unless we protect ourselves,
we may even suffer from malicious influences. The
law works in either direction. We are therefore
told in this chapter how to control life through the
control of thoughts and emotions.

IX. THE EMOTIONAL SELF AND THE CAUSES OF

DISEASE 68

It has become plain, then, that through the avenue
of thought and feeling man controls his destiny or
is subject to control from without if he allows it.
Disease can be directly traced to unguarded emotional life. The fatal effect of harsh and careless
words is thus revealed especially in the life of
women. Calamity-howlers should be fined or imprisoned as awakening the fear-thought which produces the disease or disaster. Yet we must never
blame our troubles on others, as the power is given
us to control these things by conscious choices.
We must refrain from emotions that poison the
blood, etc. We therefore study what attitude of
mind to assume in the case of psychic disease and
the subtle pains of abused love nature. Thus man
is shown his power to control life and happiness by
the thoughts he thinks and the emotions he enter-
tains. He can heal himself of every disease through
these laws.

PART TWO

BEING AS THE PERSONAL SPIRIT

pleted. We shall always be on the pathway of becoming. Proof of immortality lies here, for we cannot conceive of an end to the process any more
than we can conceive of an end to numbers. Again,
since impersonal mind creates and manifests exactly as we think, it must manifest immortality, for
we never cease to impress the concept of immortality upon it. The first law of nature is self-
preservation; and, by a common instinct, we impress this idea on impersonal mind. Thus we impress the idea of life; and it manifests as life; of
immortality and it manifests as immortality. Physical death must not be confounded with the experience of the soul. Thus death should be thought of,
not as the end of things, but as the beginning. It is
not a "taking off" but a taking on. Thus is death
swallowed up in victory by the soul that "knows
Him in whom it has believed."

We have thus discovered the law of life and mind
and our control through knowledge. *The one great
need of human thought has been shown to be the
distinct necessity of recognizing Spirit as such from
Alpha to Omega.* Then being and becoming shall be
found in their true relationship. *To know God and
the self is life eternal. Thus being has its perfect
becoming.* Our age demands that in our becoming
we reveal the true nature of Being. The marriage
of Being and Becoming is effected when the message and the messenger are one. Like Jesus, we
may appear declaring, "I am he." "I am" is being:
"I am he" is becoming. The new Messiah is he
who embodies the truth of being; and thus man
speaks while the Father dwelling in him doeth
the works.

PART I.

BEING AS THE IMPERSONAL LIFE.

CHAPTER I.

BEING OR THE CHANGELESS LIFE.

WE live in the midst of God and yet we do not know Him. Mysteries press in upon us on every hand and yet we fail to understand. A worm goes to sleep and wakes up a butterfly; an egg is warmed for three weeks in a drawer and a chicken breaks forth from its marble cell; a bullet cuts its way through shrieking flesh and internal agents restore every organ, cell for cell and nerve for nerve. A nut, an egg or a grain of sand hides within it the secret of life. To explain one of them is to explain everything. Yet how often it is looked upon either as a miracle or a fraud when a man turns the inspired eye of faith to an inner power and is lifted from the very bed of death itself, or in dire financial straits calls upon God and finds supply, or in peril by sea or land discovers a guardian angel who points out for him a star and a way. How rash we are in these days of mystery, when science has discovered that the more we know the less we know, to declare that with God any thing is impossible! And perhaps we are still more rash when we dare to pass critical

3

judgment on the use of any power, whether we call that power God or mind or consciousness or truth. No power used to lighten the burdens of life or to inspire the soul to renewed faith and effort can be anything but good. Some day all men shall know this is true and that the first and greatest of all sayings is this, "Hear, O Israel, the Lord thy God, the Lord is one and beside me there is none other." Then force, energy and life shall be found to come from a common source and whosoever shall lift the burden of another's woe and pain through the use of the forces at his command shall do the will of my Father who is in heaven.

What, then, is the wonder that lies back of a nut, an egg, or a grain of sand, a healed wound, the cure of a cancer, the demonstration of success, and the glory of an uplifted faith? We can at least get closer to the Causal Mystery even though our investigations show us more of what we do not know than what we know. And, even though abashed by what he discovers, man may still feel that "haply he knows somewhat more than he knows;" and even in the nut, the egg, and the grain of sand he may find a common factor which relates them to each other and perhaps to himself.

There is no beauty in a nut. It is simple and homely; and it would appear that a botanist could make a much finer one than nature provides. But he cannot! He can stir up the chemicals that compose it, and mould them into the shape of a nut—

but *he cannot make it grow*. There is something
in the nut which he cannot imitate; there is something in it back of which he cannot go with his
analysis. We call it the life-principle.

Where in an egg shall we find the secret of the
chicken? Not one drop of blood, nor so much as
the daintiest shadow of down would we surprise
within the shell; and were we to break through the
frail door, we should render it but an open tomb,
for even as we search its shapeless form we find
that the imprisoned splendor has escaped, carrying
its secret with it. Where was that which might
have been the tiny chick; what *was* "it," where is it,
what *is* it now? And were we to have allowed it to
grow into a body and then dissected flesh and bone,
we should never have taken unawares the sleeping
yet wakeful mystery. *Life* cannot be dissected.

The chemist dissolves the grain of sand and declares that he has solved the problem of the mineral
kingdom and discovered its law by calling it "chemical affinity." But what is chemical affinity? It
is the name of a force. The chemist does not know
what the force is; he knows only that *it is*. He
has learned something *about* it, but like the botanist
and the biologist, he has not learned *it*. The discovery of the supreme fact of its nature or law,
however, has done much for us in solving the riddle, for it has betrayed *intelligent activity*. Indeed,
something within minerals opens them to the influence of mind; and vibrations sent out at the will

of the operator can magnetize them. What is that principle within, which is thus acted upon by mind and which acts with the intelligence of mind? It is something of which again we may say, *"It is, and we know how it is; but we do not know what it is."* Yet because it betrays intelligence and because intelligence is a characteristic of mind, we may give to it a new name—*life*.

The greatest of scientists to-day are telling us that we live in a universe *alive with intelligence;* and the advanced investigator does not hesitate to declare that *all nature is alive.* But if we declare that our riddle is answered by the word *life,* what have we? We have this—that *we have reduced the universe to one;* and we have found that it is related to us in some way. *But what is "life"?*

It is a curious thing that we should thus live in a living universe; and yet not be able to tell what life is. It is one of Nature's paradoxes.

> For life we know, and knowing, do not know,
>   Yet know we whence we come, and whither go:
> For life is all, and plays the master rôle,
>   It is its own true witness to its fact:
> Illusive, subtle substance of the soul
>   That ever gives of self, and yet remains intact.

All that we can say is that *life is;* and the absence of it is what men call death. But we can go on studying *how* it acts and the law by which it is governed or by which it governs, in order that by our knowledge we may control our body and affairs.

Life is Absolute or All.

Probably the most important discovery of the new science of life is that it is universally present. We no longer think of life as being found only in some entity, here in a lily, there in a dog; but we find it everywhere, here in the stone and there in the star. There are plenty of evidences of life manifesting itself in inarticulate nature; of Life of which when we find It, we can but acknowledge the presence; we cannot say what it is. We can only say, "It Is."

The great seer, Moses, perceived the presence of this life in the flaming bush. In himself and in nature, he discovered something more than form and beauty: he found "that Something" in nature that replied to a something in himself; and communing with It, he asked, "What is your name?" He could not define this Presence; but it seemed to say, "I AM THAT I AM." "I AM" denotes life or existence; and "THAT I AM" shows that it cannot be defined in terms. But that which cannot be defined in terms must be the Absolute. Life, then, is Absolute. It is All. "The All" is found, therefore, not merely *in* nature and *in* man, but *as* nature and *as* man, and yet more than nature and man. All that we perceive is one and inseparable with it, for *all* is life. This Life is what we call Spirit.

Spirit is, therefore, Life, Mind, Intelligence, All. So anything or anyone, or all can say, "I am." "I am" comes from the verb "to be" and denotes "being." Being, therefore, indicates *that which is,* apart from time or space. It is "that which was in the beginning, is now, and ever shall be." Nor is it something outside of us. It is rather something within us which makes us what we are. It is Spirit or First Cause in us; it is that "subtle substance of the soul" coming forth into expression and manifesting as *things.* The body accordingly is spirit. We see it as body from the outside or objective point of view. But if we view it from within, it is spirit or being. So all things are *one in essence,* for all are being; and being is all or absolute.

Yet being takes "soul-form" or thought-form, so that within the lily is the eternal idea of lily which always gives birth to a lily from a lily bulb; and a rose always gives birth to a rose. Each form of life gives birth after its own kind. This is interestingly illustrated in the example of a tree. At one time, the botanist supposed that sap is drawn through the trunk and branches of a tree entirely by capillary action, that is, mechanical force. Yet it is now known that a tree will die from a shock even while its pores are unimpaired, showing that more than mechanical action is needed to explain it. In other words, there must be an *organized intelligence* within the tree which governs and sustains its life. When a shock or injury occurs, this intelligence withdraws, leaving the shell which it had built for itself to disintegrate into elemental substance again.[1]

We have here, then, sufficient evidence to show that each "living thing" in nature has a soul. We will not hesitate to say that the soul exists as the "being" of the tree, the life-principle, the thought-form, spirit acting as the idea of tree within, and taking on its body as a tree. The soul of the tree, the soul of a lily, the soul of a bird, the soul of a man, is that within which makes each thing appear in its chosen form. The soul is the individualization of spirit and shares the nature of the All-Soul. It is the life-principle and is what we call *being*. When we speak of it as One or the Whole, we call it Absolute or Eternal Being. It is eternal in essence, never changes from age to age. *It Is.*

---

[1] The elemental substance must in the nature of the case be simply disorganized thought-energy which is produced by Creative Mind as ready-made material upon which the soul-principle may draw.

CHAPTER II.

BECOMING OR THE CHANGING FORM.

WE live not only in a world of *being* but also in a world of *becoming*. Being is unfolding itself or passing itself into manifestation. In *being* is the infinite possibility; in *becoming*, this possibility is expressing. In creation, the Creator is passing into the created. Since Spirit is All, It must be the substance of all. There is nothing but Itself. In making a universe, It must fashion it out of the only material available—Itself or Being. As Being is also Mind, Its activity is that of thought; and whatever Spirit makes, It must make by passing its one essence—Mind—out into the many expressions—form—through the mould or channel—thought. To be is to think; to think is to create. Creation is eternally going on. Spirit is eternally being transformed or brought across into visible concrete substance. Or we may say that Spirit is substance which now passes into form. The growth of a lily well illustrates it. In the bulb is the *potential* form of the lily. The life-principle or soul is hidden in the bulb. At any point in the growth of the lily, two facts are cognizable. The lily has *being* or life. We can say of it, "It is." In its *being,* it is untroubled, unhurried, unworried, unshaken. It has potential power and infinite calm. But in its growth, it is also *becoming.* It is taking form and expressing beauty. Life, spirit, or being is passing into manifestation in the form of a lily. *Being is becoming* manifest. "Consider the lily," said the Great Teacher, "God clothes it."

As in the lily, so in us and in all things, there is great potential power, the power of being, while we press on to the goal of our becoming. Spirit is expressing or becoming manifest through us. It is in this way that the universal can individualize itself. It is through the recognition of the nature of the individual self that we can grasp the idea of and contact the universal. Expansion of consciousness must inevitably follow in the wake of truth.

We must rise to the glory of this truth: man is spirit, individualized into self-consciousness. God is on a glorious adventure through each of us. We are like the wave that rises on the bosom of the ocean. No matter how high or how proudly it may toss its crest, no matter what shape and form it may assume, no matter how peaceful or threatening, no matter how it may conceive itself as apart from the rest: still it lies forever on the breast of the sea, still it shares the nature and power of its source, still it is related to every other individual. There never can be any real separation in spirit.

In the end, we must recognize in each our other self. The poet recognized the truth in these words:

> "Whether the time be slow or fast,
>   Enemies hand in hand,
> Must come together at the last
>   And understand.
> No matter how the die is cast
>   Or who may seem to win,
> We know that we must love at last:
>   Why not begin?"

Thus, if we will but recognize it, we are every one of us sons of the Most High with the capacity to do all, be all, and enjoy all that heart could desire.

In practice we have but to recognize that we are in the cosmic stream of consciousness which is continuously manifesting in newer and higher forms of life, and then to allow it to become manifest for us. It is most important to note that creation is still going on; we do not live in a world that has been made; we live in a world that is being made; we live in a universe of "becoming." Nothing in nature is static; everything is in movement, change, and transition. The earth on which we dwell is forever altering, clothing and reclothing itself in garments of verdure; pouring its hidden energies out into form in the woodland violet and the giant Sequoia; emptying its sweetness in the perfume of the lily and the fragrance of the orange tree.

Just so our bodies and conditions are forever

changing; and being is becoming manifest in new ways. New life cells are born every hour. Within a year every organ and bone of the body has been born anew. Many parts of the body like the cuticle of the hand are born daily. It is literally true that

"Every day is a fresh beginning,
Every morn is the world made new:
Ye who are weary of sorrow and sinning,
Here is a beautiful hope for you—
A hope for me, and a hope for you—
EVERY DAY IS THE WORLD MADE
NEW!"

"Behold I make all things new," is the claim of the Supreme Being. "I am forever becoming manifest."

CHAPTER III.

BEING IS BECOMING THROUGH US.

THE importance of this fact must not escape us, "I—Absolute Being or Spirit—make." Man does not have to make; Spirit makes. "I will work and who can hinder it!" The inner principle of all life, plant or planet, animal or man, is forever producing; and it may be called into expression in our lives. "Behold I stand at the door and knock; if any man will open, I will come in." "Spirit *seeks* its worshipers." The creative process is going on in you. "Stand still and behold the salvation of your God." What a relief from struggle! You do not need to lie awake at night saying to the heart, "Beat seventy-two times a minute:" to the lungs, "Take a breath now;" to the blood, "Go 'round and 'round." All this is the involuntary functioning of the life in you, under the direction of the inner mind. So, too, we do not need to say, "I must make a new cell where this one is worn out: I must make a little more gastric juice to digest this food." Man does not have to create; he merely allows spirit to manifest its innate power, to permit being to become through him.

14

This spirit is in you now ready to do whatever is necessary for your health and supply. You are at one with all being, and within you is the All-Power ready to act.

> "Then go not thou in search of him,
>   But to thyself repair;
> Wait thou within the silence dim
>   And thou shalt find him there."

All great healing is done on the basis of this realization, that *the work is being done for us.* We are not forced to "hold thoughts," repeat denials, or make affirmations until the brain begins to stagger. To do this is to pass the struggle over from physical to mental gymnastics. If we are to stop beating the body, cracking the bones, boiling in mud, taking electric shocks, only to "do" our denials, affirm our affirmations, and count the rosary of our formulated phrases, with any idea that *we* are doing the job, we might as well quit now. Remember Moses! "He said unto them, 'Hear, now, ye rebels; shall *we* bring you forth water out of this rock?' And Moses lifted up his hand, and smote the rock with his rod twice: and water came forth abundantly; and the congregation drank and their cattle. And Jehovah said unto Moses and Aaron, 'Because ye believed not in *me,* to honor *me* in the eyes of the children of Israel; therefore ye shall not bring this assembly into the land which I have given them.' "

We are entered into truth to find peace; and, if we struggle along on the basis that we must do the work, we can never enter the promised land. One woman said, "I have discovered I have seven bodies; and I am trying to subdue them; but life is a constant struggle. I subdue them one by one; but by the time I get the seventh put under, the first is all up in arms." Another was asked by her friends to join in some activities; but she said, "I have no time for such things: I must go and do my denials and affirmations." I have seen people absolutely bewildered by the effort to *heal themselves* by "holding the right thought;" and I have often heard metaphysicians say, "I will *work* for you," as though there were something they had to *do*. As a matter of fact, "we do not have to struggle, we only have to know." The poet truly said,

"I am not fighting my fight,
 I am singing my song."

Said Jesus, "Can a man, by taking *thought,* add one cubit to his stature?" Of course not. Neither denials nor affirmations are *creative.* We should carefully distinguish between the terms, creative thought and creative mind. Strictly speaking, thought does not create: mind creates. The creative function is still going on; Creative Mind is building *for us;* spirit is passing into manifestation, being is becoming; we do not have to struggle, but rather do we say to the God within,

"Build me more stately mansions, O *my soul.*"

What we need to do is to recognize the presence of the spiritually-perfect being, which we are; and thus allow it to become, which it will do!

THE FAITH OF A CHILD.

Thought itself, then, does not create. Creation goes on without our conscious thought; and conscious thought simply acts as a mould to spirit as it passes through. This is why a child's life is normally so healthy and serene. It does not put up any barrier to the flow of pure spirit. It does not interpose fear or doubt. It takes all on faith; and the creative impulse goes on to build its growing body and fill its heart with joy. A friend of mine, who was a teacher in one of the grade schools, had a lame wrist and felt herself unable to get the right thought about it. So she went to a little five-year-old boy in her room and said, "John, I hear that you healed Miss So-and-So's finger? Do you think you could heal my wrist?" "Yes, teacher, let me hold it." So he took the wrist between his little hands and sat silent for a moment. "It will be all right, now," he said. And it was healed immediately. Other cases might be cited in which children have demonstrated the power of unreasoning faith. Among some of our acquaintances, the whole family depends on the faith of one of the children. Whenever sickness occurs, they all turn to the boy or girl. The faith of a little child is the faith that sees *God at work for us*, bearing our burdens, providing for our necessities, living in His creation, a Presence in everything, working for our good. To realize this is the acme of spiritual understanding. "No evil shall befall thee, neither shall any plague come nigh thy dwelling. He shall give his angels charge over thee to keep thee in all thy ways." Being is becoming; that which is unmanifest is becoming manifest; and, as it is perfect in being, it must also be perfect in becoming, if we will but recognize the truth of being and become fit channels for its expression. For we are individuals; and spirit can become for us only in the measure of our choice and channel. Ours it is to open or shut the door to Spirit.[1]

How we may assume the attitude of mind that will assure the most perfect expression of spirit in our bodies, affairs, and states of consciousness, we shall study in succeeding chapters. Let us here open our thought to the influx of spirit as faith.

I do rest in the calm assurance that all that the Father hath is mine. I know that "beneath me are the girders of the Almighty and underneath are the Everlasting Arms." "The Lord is my light and my salvation, whom shall I fear? The Lord is the strength of my life, of whom [or what] shall I be afraid?" "My Father is greater than I." I

---

[1]This is not to be construed in any way as opposing the right use of affirmations.

will "rest in the Lord and wait patiently for Him."
"I will look unto the hills from whence cometh our
help; my help cometh from the Lord which makes
heaven and earth." I do now answer the command
of my soul, "Come unto me all ye that labor and
are heavy-laden; and I will give you rest." Father,
I rest my case in thy hands and now know that
thou wilt give me fully and freely this thing which
I seek.

CHAPTER IV.

THE MENTAL UNIVERSE—WHY WE CALL THINGS IDEAS.

THE first principle of life is this, "I am or being." All human knowledge begins here. It is not a matter of proof but of intuition. I know that I am. And if I do not know that I am, I do not know anything, for there is no one to know it. And I also know that this "I am" is a self. I reach this conclusion by the necessary observation that the "I am" which I know I am is different in many respects from others around me. So that I know that I am *a self;* that is, I have a life which I myself direct, and of which I myself am conscious. At the same time, I realize that, in some subtle way, this self is related to all selves and all being because being must be one, as we have already seen. Again, since being is all, the life that manifests everywhere must be the life of the One. I cannot get away from the fact, therefore—and I do not wish to—that *each thing that I see about me is an expression of that Being.* A thing is the form in which Spirit embodies itself as an individual entity, as we saw in the case of the tree in Chapter One. Nor can we get away from the fact that Mind, since it is the substance out of which everything is made as well as the intelligence that makes it, can assume any form of self-expression which it desires. It is probable, therefore, that I may say of the tree just as I say of myself, it is a self. There is doubtless a tree-self, just as there is a man-self.[1]

Finally, we may speak in general terms of the thing as an *idea* of spirit. Since Spirit is Mind and since Mind acts by thought, anything that it brings forth must be a thought creation and therefore an idea. It is true that it would be more than what we ordinarily think of as an idea, for it acts with a definite intelligence; and it would be far more perfect language to say that the tree, for example, is God thinking the thought of "tree" and then *becoming* the tree which He thinks. For that is the way that Being expresses itself, it becomes the thing which it thinks and therefore makes. And in the case of all form and life, we find that Being does not become hurriedly; but, by some process of growth from within, it finally unfolds its nature along the line of the idea which it has conceived itself to be. So that the term "idea" is very useful in the language of the newer thought because it expresses two aspects of each thing: first, the presence of mind within it, for mind acts by ideas

[1]Compare page 456, Calkin's *Persistent Problems of Philosophy.*

or concepts, that is, by thinking; second, definiteness of thought, for each *form* must necessarily have a definite thought back of it, or it would not come forth in form at all. *We may think, then, of each thing in nature as being embodying itself in a definite idea as a definite self.*

When we learn to look upon the world in this way, we enter into a new and different life, for we no longer see inanimate nature and the cold and colorless forms of matter; but *we see and feel the vibrant presence of the Spirit of Life Itself.* Each thing is being assuming form and coming forth for expression. The flower has a voice eloquent of God; the sunset betrays his glory in brilliant colors; and the friendly stars are the lamps our Father sets to guide our feet aright. Each thing that we see, be it the reef or rock or the rippling tide, the shrilling cricket or the roaring lion, is revealed as Spirit embodying Itself as an idea. We live in a universe of intelligence, a mental world, wherein everything that we taste, touch, smell, see or hear is an idea of being.

And all this will show us how man may control the affairs of his life, once he shall perceive his own relationship to the cosmic order and his own power as a self to control his ideas and those lesser intelligences by which he finds himself surrounded. We must therefore turn our attention next to a study of the close relationship between all selves and ideas.

THE UNITY IN NATURE.

I think that nothing more fully shows the unity of creation and the Oneness of the Mind that puts it forth than the fact of the dependence of each thing on other things for its own self-expression. Take for example the tree. Being is here individualizing itself on the idea of tree. The tree is a distinct life-form and has an individual selfhood. It is an entity and maintains a separate existence, yet see what it shares with the whole? It puts out a form to fit its environment. If it is in a valley where it has plenty of freedom, see with what lofty self-confidence it rears its proud head and spreads its sweeping branches. If, however, it springs from a seed, carelessly scattered by some mighty giant in a forest of giants, the young sapling makes its way timorously and unobtrusively to the light until, in the process of centuries, it may at last itself become a king. If in the pathway of the winds, the young oak sets its roots deeply and defiantly exposes its sturdy branches to the sweeping gale.

Again, the very *color* of a tree, it must borrow, as it were, from all nature. It has no color apparently within itself, but catches the rays of the sun, absorbing some, reflecting others and taking on just that shade that befits its own particular idea. Nor is the *idea* of color *entirely* within the tree itself, for it must depend upon the mind of the observer for the full effect of its beauty. That the tree can never be a fully-expressed idea without other selves outside of it, to appreciate it, can be shown by a simple illustration. If I "look" at a tree, what do I "see"? Certain vibrations in the ether (which is the physical science name for Mind) passing as light to my eye, impinge upon the surface, causing another set of vibrations to pass through the eye and down the optic nerve to a brain-center. Here they cause a cell-explosion or vibration. At the same moment and because of it, I have a mental image or subjective vision of a tree. And the rose which appears to me to be upon the tree sends forth a particular vibration which I detect and I say, "It is red." But it is not the red in the rose but the idea of red awakened by the vibration which I myself "see." Again, I say it has an odor; but as a matter of fact, I get the vibration; and my mind interprets it as perfume. I touch it and say that it is cool because the vibration that is awakened in me suggests the idea of coolness.

OUR OWN THOUGHT NECESSARY TO THE FULL MEANING OF THINGS.

So I might go on to show that all nature and things are united with every other person and thing and dependent for their full perfection and expression of the idea upon other things and minds. They are not appreciable without a mind to appreciate them. They do not have heat, cold, sound, odor, color, nor taste of themselves. These are names which we give to varying degrees of vibration which we interpret according to our own idea.

It has been necessary to speak of this because all the so-called modern movements, whether Christian Science, Divine Science, or New Thought, base their teachings, and rightly, on true scientific principles, the fact that we live in a world of ideas. "The physicists teach us that there is nothing in the physical world exactly corresponding to the different colors, sounds, degrees of heat and cold, flavors and odors of the natural world as we know it. Colors and the rest, they teach, are mere ideas; and the 'real causes' of these ideas are forms of vibration."[2]

Thus, referring back to the tree, we find that the idea which is there in the form of a tree is Being become manifest in vibrations of varying degrees of intensity which radiate in every direction, awakening in the minds of those who behold it the idea of color, perfume, and beauty. And the tree-self is related to all other selves and is never complete apart from those selves. All nature is interrelated in the same way. The cloud depends upon the mist, the mist upon the sea, the sea on the brook and the rain, and the rain on the cloud. So that life moves forever round in the circle of the All-Mind.

[2]Calkin's *Persistent Problems of Philosophy,* page 121.

The spring is mated to the brook
　　In one continuous flow;
The sky is mated to the sea
　　In one long crimson glow;
The mountains melt into the mist,
　　And, stretching rise on rise,
They range afar to yonder star
　　And mix in star-dust skies.

The star is mirrored in the spring,
　　Its spirit mated there:
And thus the great round circle runs
　　To link the everywhere.
'Tis love that winds through things and minds
　　In one long, golden chain;
O'er circles vast, love's loop is cast,
　　And all is *one* again.

Each thing is incomplete without every other, just as a word is incomplete without the sentence or the letter without the word. And as words have no meaning without a mind to assemble and cognize them, so there must be a mind to assemble all these factors in the expression of any one idea and to perceive each thing as a whole or entity or self. This is the wonderful function of the individual mind, even of the animal, for it doubtless gets impressions similar to, though not so wonderful as, our own.

CHAPTER V.

IF "THINGS ARE IDEAS," WHAT IS "REAL"?

IT is plain that as each thing or idea depends for its full-rounded expression upon the mind that perceives it, as we have already seen; then a question might arise as to whether there is, after all, anything there for us to cognize. If we all see colors differently; if coolness, softness, odors, and even forms and vibrations look different to each of us (and they do to a certain degree) what factor of the idea remains permanent? Is there a "Thing-in-Itself"? Is not everything after all an illusion, and is not all the world in our own minds? I suspect that this question will sound stupid to the average person, and well it may; yet so vexing is the problem of reality that the tallest minds have often lost their bearings here, and have become space-wanderers while the mind that judges everything on the face of it has by an instinct of nature kept what must, in the light of present understanding of the universe, come to be regarded as the truer path. But let us ask and answer the question, that we may see why we call *things* real and not illusions.

We have already seen that Being or Mind is the substance of all and that in creation we find Being becoming manifest or expressed. Life would not be at all if it could not act or create. Creation is the form taken by God's thought. Recognizing God or the inner principle of all as Mind, co-extensive with infinity, we perceive that its only method of action is mental, that is, by thought. So whatever expression Being has, is by thought. But *we always find the thought or expression in the form of vibration,* so *that we know that thought is vibration, force or energy.*[1]

It is also by no means impossible that that which we call Being, Mind or Cosmic Consciousness is itself of the same nature as vibration. In other words, consciousness or vibration is at once the material of God and the universe. If this be so, then in the act of what we call creation, the only thing that would be necessary would be to lower the rate of vibration at any chosen point when it would become what we call "matter." The thought of Creative Mind would then mould this substance into form. In that case, we have no problem at all as to how the transition takes place from mind to thought or vibration, since both are one. This would do away with the whole question of illusions since whatever we "see," etc., would be the ultimate real itself, or God in individual form.

---

[1]Read Chapter VIII, "Matter or Thought in Form," in my book, *The Law of Mind in Action.*

At any rate, vibration, or thought, is the substance of the visible universe, since the atom is but a composite of energy. Matter is therefore thought in form, which in turn can be recognized only by mind. Man is aware of that which we call matter or physical substance only through the activity of consciousness. In other words, the energy resident in matter produces in our mind a series of psychic shocks which we translate into an interpretation of matter as sound, color, odor, and so on.

It is a fact, then, that the basis of matter is also the basis of consciousness, for both are Being in process of expression or vibration. When, therefore, I "see" anything I am perceiving the thought of the Creator and interpreting it through my mind which is akin to His. In other words, there is something *real* outside of my individualized mind; but I can cognize it only because it is related to my mind, since it and I are in the One Mind; and it is an idea or thought appealing to me.

Let us illustrate the principle in the case of a rose. Suppose I say, "I see a rose," and then close my eyes and say, "I do not see the rose." The rose disappears from my vision. If I open my eyes again, the rose reappears. What is it that appears and disappears? Certainly it is the mental image or subjective vision of the rose which appears and disappears. Apparently there remains something which is outside my own conscious thinking, which does not so quickly appear and disappear, for there is the presence there of something which awakened my attention to itself: and my friends see a rose in the same place and at various times without my calling their attention to it.

WHAT IS REAL?

The question is, which is *real*, the objective rose which stimulates attention, or the subjective vision or correspondent, or both, or neither? The answer is not difficult in the light of what we have already said. Things are thoughts; and the source is mind or consciousness. Mind puts forth its thought clothed in form. Here the thought has appeared as a rose: but a thought is vibration and so is a rose. On the objective side is the vibration and form which my physical senses caught up and recorded; on the subjective side there is the awakening in my consciousness of my idea of a rose. That idea has always been there because it is a part of the absolute consciousness; but up to the moment of my seeing the rose, my consciousness was, as it were, asleep on that point. The *vibration* from *the objective rose* is *thought* awakening a mental correspondent in my mind, by the association of ideas. Hence I *see* the rose. Now the "I" that sees or cognizes the rose *perceives it as a thought or idea.* There is no difficulty to be experienced in understanding the process by which the outer idea stimulates the inner idea, when we realize that the rose, and I, and my subjective idea of a rose which is the

symbol that appeared to me, alike exist in the One
Consciousness. Accordingly I recognize the rose
as not my idea alone but as an idea or thought of
the Infinite which is put forth in a form to be seen
by all individual minds, and which has, therefore, *an
entity separate from my own mind or thought.* It
is recognizable to me because I am a thinker; and
it is a thought. In this way and because there is
about the objective rose a persistency and stability
which awakens in every one who sees it the idea
of a rose, I can tell the difference between my
mere fancies or hallucinations and reality. There
stands forth in the rose a residue of something
apart from *my* ideas of color, smell, or feeling. *It
is the idea of the Infinite Himself.*

Illusions.

We have thus seen that the rose—like, of course,
all other sensible objects—exists not only in my
mind but also in the Divine Mind as an idea clothed
in form, and is therefore independent of my idea
of it, to the extent that it would persist if my individual consciousness were withdrawn from it.
It is true that the full beauty and wonder of creation would never be realized without an individual
mind to reclothe it in living colors; yet it does not
depend for its existence upon that mind. It is
even conceivable that the Divine Mind that sets it
forth in space as a vibrant form may perceive it
as we do, not devoid of color, warmth, and sweet-

ness, but rather with a finer beauty and fragrance than we can conceive; and there it stands forth until the Mind withdraws the thought. It is thus that we must consider the splendor of a sunset, the majestic volume of the Nile, and the flaming comet: they would still be, even as they must have been, before the advent of man.

They would still be

> That mystic, magic wonder, mountain and sea,
>   Made by the thought of Him who sits aloft,
> Who joys in flower and tree.

It is, therefore, a mistake to speak of the common experiences of mankind as illusions and to say that we live in a world of illusions. It is true that we do not live in a world of matter, using the word matter as meaning that which is independent of consciousness; but the objects by which we find ourselves surrounded are real objects since they are the thoughts and substance of the Ultimate Real, or God. To call them an illusion is to say that we suppose ourselves to perceive something, when in reality that thing does not exist at all. This is absurd, for if there were no real thing then there would be nothing to call my attention to it and the mere fancies of my day-dreams would be as real as my perceptions of that which common experience declares to be of more value at least; an imaginary dollar would be as good as a coined one. Yet you couldn't buy a pound of sugar with an imaginary

dollar. To say that things are illusions is mental suicide, because it makes all experiences unreal, de-
stroys the veracity of the mind, declares that reason is not dependable, and that the conclusions of
the reason cannot be depended upon. Then whatever the reason declares would also be not dependable; and the proclamation that we live in a world
of illusion would be itself an illusion. The doctrine of illusions leads more quickly along the pathway of pure idiocy than anything else of which I
happen to know.

On the contrary, to say that the thing is thought
in form, and as such has reality, is to live in a
world peopled with commonsense entities, and living, vital, real ideas. Things are thoughts or ideas,
and are real, because in essence and nature they are
a part of consciousness.

.   .   .   .   .   .

CONTROL OF LIFE THROUGH THOUGHTS AND IDEAS.

The value of this study must not be overlooked.
Its purpose is to lead us to realize more perfectly
our relationship to the universe and the power which
we may exercise over things because they are ideas.
Back of everything we see is the thought or mind
that brought it into expression. On the subjective
side of life, I am one with the Eternal Thinker,
and share to a certain extent His consciousness of
everything. That is why I can understand what I
see, because I am related to Him who made them,

and deep seated in my mystic frame is the mind that can know and interpret all. Moreover through this relationship, I may bring to pass the things *I* desire to be changed or done. For I can set up ideas of my own in the One Mind; and the Creative Principle will act upon them. I control, then, through my subjective relationship to the All. I choose what I shall do through my objective faculties which give me my individuality. Therefore let us declare for ourselves this truth:

I live in a world wherein everything is thought in form; it is the idea of Mind; and in everything breathes the presence of God. I live and have my being in this All-Conscious One and share His nature and life. I understand Him; and He understands me. I accept His gifts and dare to call upon Him for all that my heart can crave. I feel the vastness of His nature and the reality of His Selfhood, for were He less than person He could not put forth the ideas which thrill me with the mystery and wonder of life. I worship before the Beauty of His nature expressed in the colorful tintings of the things I see: His majesty in the mountains: His Harmonious Soul in the song of the brooks and the birds: His tenderness in the love of every mating and mothering thing. All these things are His ideas; and great indeed is the marvel of that Nature that puts them forth. Like to me He is, for we can understand each other's ideas. I therefore rest in quiet confidence in His

power to act; and the Love that moves Him both
to provide for my necessities and to carry me over
the rough places of life.

> Be still, for I thy Father dwell
>   Within thine inmost soul:
> Be still and let my Voice command
>   Thy heart, my Word control
> Thine act: oh, rest in quiet 'til
>   My thought shall rule thy will.

CHAPTER VI.

PERSONAL AND IMPERSONAL MIND.

ALL nature is vibrant with the presence of Being bursting into expression in the flowering bush, the flitting butterfly, the flaming sunrise and the raging torrent. Each thing is Being clothing itself in its own ideas. It is God's thought expressed in the language of form and beauty and sustained by the presence of the spirit embodied in it. Each thing that we see may be regarded as a self in the truest meaning of the word: not, it is true, with a developed self-consciousness as in human life, but having, nevertheless, some kind of sensational and emotional experience, a true entity carrying out some *definite purpose* for which it came into manifestation as an entity.

We cannot, if we would, get away from the fact that Being acts as a self in each individual thing and person, for *all* is one; and therefore this one must be in each individual thing. The distinction between persons and things largely disappears in the light of the allness of Being, and becomes merely a difference in the type, purpose, or self-consciousness of the varied forms, whether plant, animal or man. Such an understanding must make the universe very personal to us and take from us the fear we once entertained of the so-called impersonal forces of nature. With some truth, we may exclaim with the star-gazer,

> For I am part of Him
>   That made thee shine;
> And through the spaces dim
>   And ether fine,
> I claim thee on the rim
>   Of heav'n as mine:
> My star, my light, my beam,
>   You shine for me;
> And, in your radiant beam,
>   The light I see
> Of Him that made thee shine—
>   'Tis God and thee.[1]

We therefore see Being everywhere acting as the personal spirit with emotional life and powers of self-direction. At the same time, we should clearly discriminate between the personal and the impersonal activity of Mind, else we shall be falling into all the old errors of thought wherein we shall ever be at cross purposes with a Will and Mind opposed to our own. For this reason it is well for us to study the other aspect of Mind, the impersonal. And we can find no better illustration than in the study of the individual himself.

---

[1] *Songs of the Silence*, by the author.

THE PERSONAL MIND OF THE INDIVIDUAL.

Each of us has a mind which acts in two ways,
personal and impersonal. The personal mind each
of us is familiar with. This is the mind that
chooses, intellectualizes, and wills. It selects the
objects of its desire and plans and purposes what
it will do. It conceives ideas and insists on their
fulfilment. In the individual, this aspect of mind
is often spoken of as objective, while the impersonal side of mind is often spoken of as subjective. The objective mind, as we know it in the individual, is largely the aspect of mind which he
develops to contact an objective environment. The
babe is born into the world practically subjective,
that is, acting without conscious thought or choice.
But so soon as the child begins to react to environment, it needs an individualization of mind to meet
life's emergencies. This it develops. When it
learns that a cry will give it nourishment, a yell
will give it a rattle, and the word "papa" will give
it anything, it has begun the development of an
objective mind. This is the mind with which we
are all familiar in the sprightly intercourses of
life, wherein man plans, works and struggles. But
while it seems to be the outgrowth of man's objective necessities, we must never think of it as at all
separate from the *one* mind which the individual
has, for all objective faculties lie latent in subjective mind; and it is only because it is potentially

there that man can develop it at all. The personal *self*, then, is simply the emergence into formal expression of the personal *spirit* which each one of us is. It is the consciousness of a self as apart from other selves and persons, to the extent that each knows he is an individual who chooses and wills as a distinct self.

THE IMPERSONAL MIND OF THE INDIVIDUAL.

On the other hand, there is an activity of mind in each of us which may be classed as impersonal. It is to be discovered in the unconscious process by which we govern the breathing, the circulation of the blood, the birth of new life cells and the rejection of old ones which we pass automatically through the pores of the body, the kidneys, and so on. It is the phase of mind that acts while we sleep, standing guard at the ear to open it to the incoming of some sounds and to close it to others. The peaceful ticking of the clock, the rattle of the window-pane, or the familiar snore of our companion, it gracefully turns away from our conscious attention; but should a burglar pry at the window or one of the children cry for water, at once the subjective mind opens the doorway of the conscious attention; and we are aroused from our slumbers.

This is the mind that can hear without ears and see without eyes, as has been abundantly proven in recent years by experiments of various kinds. Messages can be conveyed to it and from it to other minds without the aid of mechanical agencies by the process of what is known as thought-transference or mental telepathy. Apparently everything that ever enters the storehouse of its memory is kept there without loss, although it may never again step out onto the threshold of objective consciousness. It is the phase of mind through which our intuitions are brought to us and registered upon our attention. Here we scatter the seeds of our ambitions and ideas; and, in the rich soil of the mind, these ideas take root and grow into purposes and plans. Thus genius, seeking expression in beautiful forms, dreams the dream in the stillness of the mind within; and at length the perfected idea springs forth in the glory of the chiseled form.

Whatever falls upon the rich soil of this mind is bound to bear fruit of some kind, for with tireless activity it goes to work to "think out" for us the things we are puzzling over, to show us the best way to go, to act both as teacher and servant for us. It is significant that this is the mind that has charge of all growth, whether it be in the budding and bloom of genius, in the development of the full-rounded purpose, or in the reconstruction of the body through the creation of new cells.

There is surely enough here to betoken the *infinite and eternal heritage of the mind within us*. What mind is this that never forgets, that creates out of the raw material of the unseen the noblest that has

sprung into form through human genius, that loves
to the edge of the grave and beyond, that builds
and molds and fashions the human frame in continuous growth? These are attributes of a vaster
intelligence, not earth- but heaven-born. For, as
noted in previous chapters, *we have perceived in
nature herself the same creative intelligence in active operation.* This is the impersonal activity of
the Universal Mind.

IMPERSONAL MIND ACTS ONLY ON IDEAS "GIVEN" TO IT.

But just why do we call it impersonal? We call
it impersonal because it is not the phase of mind
that *chooses* what shall come to pass. *The personal mind chooses what it shall have and then
passes its orders over to the impersonal mind to
execute.* In the individual, this is well illustrated
in the case of a hypnotized person. In this state,
the subject loses his consciousness of personality
and takes on the personality of the operator. Instead of making selections of ideas for himself, *he
takes whatever idea is given to him* and begins to
act upon that. If he is told that he is a great singer,
he tries to sing. If told that he is a great sculptor,
he tries to mold and chisel. If told that on the
following day at 12:01, he will pull out his watch
and wind it, he takes that idea and the next day,
to his own personal astonishment, the impersonal
mind carries out the idea that was impressed upon

it; and he winds his watch in the public market, or wherever he may chance to be.

THE UNIVERSAL IMPERSONAL.

However, we must not make the mistake of conceiving of a personal mind apart from the impersonal, for *the personal can rise into individuality only out of the impersonal;* and to conceive of a personal separate from the impersonal would lead us to attempt to accomplish things by human will and force alone. And this again would lead to a universe of many minds, God's mind and each of ours, and thus to eternal conflicts of purpose and consequent turmoil. *Nor should we ever conceive of an impersonal mind apart from a personal.* This would lead to the assumption that the universe is one merely of mechanical force, and thus to materialism, atheism, and ignorance. Back of all personal expressions of life must be that from which they spring. And, as Being, from its very nature of being "That-which-Is," must be One, the impersonal life of the individual must share in that Being or Life; and the personal life of each of us must rest eternally back on the one source of all.

⁘   •   •.   ⦂•⦂   ⦂•⦂   ⦂•⦂

PERSONALIZING THE UNIVERSAL IMPERSONAL.

The Famous "Talking Horses."

We can find illustrations of the direct relation-

ship of the individual forms of life and the universal in plants, animals, and man. I think however that science has never had so startling a proof
of what metaphysics has long taught as can be
found in the trained horses of Elberfeld. I confess that I cannot write of them without such a
thrill as one experiences only in presence of a great
mystery, for though science has admitted that these
horses actually do perform the wonders which I
relate, still we must recall that the back of everything we know is as great a mystery as the face of
everything we do not know.

The horses in question were trained by a man
named Krall; and the genuineness of their per-
formances is attested by an imposing list of leading scientists of several countries. Various theories
have been advanced as to the source of the intelligence of these animals; but no reputable scientist
now questions the fact of the intelligence itself.
The facts are these: A system of numbers is ar-
ranged in such a way that the horses will know
that a certain number of blows with the foot will
represent each figure. For instance, following the
English method of numbers, twenty-four would be
represented first by two blows, and then four. A
certain number of blows also represents each letter
of the alphabet so that the horse can spell out any
word that he may desire. With this simple ma-
chinery of language and without the aid of a voice,
the horses perform prodigies of intelligence that

are more than marvelous. Asked to multiply 24
by 7 for example, the horse will strike out the reply with instantaneous quickness and apparently
without any conscious calculation. The horses have
been taught how to extract the square root of numbers and can extract it instantly from any number
that gives an exact root. Not only this, but also
without having been taught to solve any number
beyond the square root of 144, the horses can extract the cube root of any number and even the
fourth root.

When Maeterlinck visited the stables at Elberfeld, he was introduced by Krall to Muhamed, one
of the horses; and the horse was asked to spell
Maeterlinck's name, which he accomplished with
little difficulty. To prove that there was no collu-
sion on account of a previous knowledge of his
visit, Maeterlinck remained with Muhamed alone
and asked him to spell the name of his hotel "Wei-
denhof." This the animal did.

One day Zarif (another of the horses) suddenly
stopped in the midst of his lessons. They asked
him the reason.

"Because I am tired."

Another time he answered: "Pain in my leg."

One day Krall and his collaborator, Dr. Scheller,
thought that they would try to teach Muhamed to
express himself in speech. The horse, a docile and
eager pupil, made touching and fruitless efforts to

reproduce human sounds. Suddenly he stopped;
and, in his strange phonetic spelling, declared, by
striking his foot on the spring board:

"I have not a good voice."

Observing that he did not open his mouth, they
strove to make him understand, by the example of
a dog, with pictures, and so on, that, in order to
speak, it is necessary to separate the jaws. They
next asked him:

"What must you do to speak?"

He replied by striking with his foot:

"Open the mouth."

"Why don't you open yours?"

"Because I can't."

I thus quote directly from Maeterlinck's *Unknown Guest* because he personally examined the
case of the horses and because, after a study of all
theories designed to account for such astonishing
intelligence, he comes to the conclusion that *the
horses are the instrument through which a vaster
intelligence articulates.* The theory of signs im-
perceptible to the onlooker had to be abandoned
because one of the horses, Berto, is blind and could
not detect such signs. Nor is it what we call mental
telepathy, for, as Maeterlinck amusingly relates, he
himself did not know the answer to some of the
problems he proposed, while examining the horse
alone in the stable, and more than that *he never had
known,* and did not even know where nor how to

get it.   How then could the horse read it from his mind?   Other experiments also have been made to show that it is not telepathy.

By a series of experiments and deductions into which we cannot go here, since space does not permit, and which the student or skeptic can examine for himself to better advantage in the book above mentioned, Maeterlinck comes to the conclusion that we can *attribute the almost superhuman intelligence of the horses only to a subliminal consciousness, which is in touch with the immediate answer to every problem.*   Like the mathematical prodigies of history who have been able to calculate numbers without the aid of rules and by some immediate process, the horses seem to read the answer from some cosmic page.   Such an explanation seems also necessary to explain the quickness which they exhibit in learning words and their meanings, for in a few weeks they learn what a child must take a long time to acquire in the use of language.   Maeterlinck concludes that either we must attribute to the horse an intelligence which challenges belief as beyond that of ordinary human powers or else, "we should have to admit that there is in the horse —and hence most probably in everything that lives on this earth—a psychic power similar to that which is hidden beneath the veil of our reason and which, as we learn to know it, astonishes, surpasses and dominates our reason more and more.   *This psychic power, in which no doubt we shall one day be forced to recognize the genius of the universe itself, appears, as we have often observed, to be all-wise, all-seeing, and all-powerful.* It has, when it is pleased to communicate with us or when we are allowed to penetrate into it, an answer for every question and perhaps a remedy for every ill." [2]

I have not quoted here in order to establish Maeterlinck's opinion as an authority; but I have presented the facts as he found them; and the reader can judge for himself. For my part, I see here but another evidence of the truth that *there is but one Mind functioning through many individuals,* expressing in many things, embodying in many ideas. This is simply another of those scientific evidences of the principles of mental science which are daily coming to hand.

We see then that the individualized consciousness, at the deeper points of its current, mingles freely with the subterranean stream from which it instinctively draws and by which it is fed and sustained either wittingly or unwittingly. The individualized mind, forgetful of its origin, engrossed in the affairs and complications of an objective world, loses its consciousness of the all-embracing wisdom, and seldom floats to the surface the pure ideas from the profound and placid depths. Yet there come moments in life when some storm smites the surface; and we quiver to the depth of our being. It is then that pure intuitions come to us;

---

[2]The italics are mine.

and we see with startling vision; we know with
supernatural clearness; we understand without the
processes of reason. Something rises up within us
to take possession, leading us out of peril, giving
us "the strength of madness," inspiring us to the
necessary action, acting as the creative genius and
the ruling spirit that masters every power that
threatens. And woe to that man or society that
stands in the path of the God-inspired soul, for he
announces divinity; and in him God Himself is
marching onward to his triumph!

INDIVIDUAL CHOICE WITHIN THE IMPERSONAL MIND.

We are thus brought face to face with the great
mystery, *God in man,* or as a great seer once said,
"Christ in you the hope of glory." Thus, by plunging beneath the surface of his ordinary consciousness, man finds that he does not enter another sea,
for he finds no break between the surface and the
profoundest depths. He is related to the All, not
by proximity nor contact, but in actual nature and
being. Man does not leave off where God begins.
If he will but realize this and seek to establish
relationship in conscious thought, where alone separation of any kind is possible, he cannot but feel
and know that back of him is the power and the
life of the All, and that he is entitled to *act as the
personal factor* within that Life. In other words
as it stands back of us as the impersonal basis of

our own life, it is our right and privilege to impress upon it the ideas and desires which our own personal life demands. And since it takes each idea and goes to work to produce in visible form the invisible thought which has been given it, we may be sure that it cannot fail to bring forth for us whatever we may desire.

Thus do we have outlined for ourselves the principle of mind. There is one universal, all-comprehensive Mind having the power to choose what it shall create, and to initiate its own ideas, and thus to act as a Person or Self: while at the same time it is an impersonal force or creative energy building for us "whatsoever things we ask in faith believing." For as we are in this One Mind and our own individuality arises from it, we may make personal choices of what we shall have; and it will body them forth for us.

One may well rest back in a sense of quiet security upon the assurance that these truths afford. Let us say: I am one with the infinite intelligence; and the infinite energy is back of every word I speak and every desire that I voice. I may ask what I will in the name of my inner and real self; and it shall be done unto me of my Father. Father, I will that thou shalt open to me the storehouses of a diviner wisdom that I may walk in the pathway of truth and learn more to enjoy the companionship of the Ever-Present One whom Thou art.

I am thy life within thee,
I am thy health;
I am thy choicest treasure;
I am thy wealth.
I am thy deepest wisdom;
I am thy light;
I am thy power within thee;
I am thy might:
I am thy warm emotion;
I am thy truth;
I am thy ageless heritage;
I am thy youth;
I am thy hope of heaven;
I am the way;
I am the light eternal;
I am the day:
I am thy will-to-conquer;
I am thy sword;
I am the peace thou cravest;
I am thy word.

   . . . . . .

I am the Inner Presence,
Forever nigh:—
Whenever thou dost say, "I am,"
I Am That I.[3]

---

[3]From *Songs of the Silence,* by the author.

CHAPTER VII.

THE PART "I" PLAY IN COSMIC MIND.

THE farthest advance of God into self-expression is in each one of us. We must learn
to realize the wonderful part we play in the
great plan. You and I are purposes of God, for
through us He is coming constantly into great adventures and new experiences. It would not be
like being a God at all, unless every possible experience could be enjoyed by Him. As the Absolute Being without individuality, God could not
have the delightful experiences we have as individuals. For He could not know what it is to love
without a lover; He could not know what it is to
enjoy the suspense of the future, since in the Absolute there is no sense of time; He could not know
what it is to enjoy a journey, since in the Absolute
there is no space; He could not carry out the joy
of logical or inductive thinking, since with the Absolute everything is known at once. But God would
not be God unless He had the ability to do all of
these things and have every kind of experience.
Thus He ventures forth as an individual, and becomes a self.

You and I are this self. Remember we are not all of God though all that we are is God. The Absolute could not be confined in the individual; but the individual may go on expanding endlessly toward the Absolute. If, then, we will but realize our relationship to God, we may go on in the sense of a wonderful purpose and a marvelous nature. Through us, God is writing the story of life; through us, He is the poet who dreams the dream of beauty; through us, He sculptures the marble; through us, He plans the building; through us hews the stone; through us, He does the commonplace work of the world; through us, He cheers another soul; through us loves with love surpassing human understanding. If mothers are not God on earth, then God is neither in heaven nor earth. Says Kipling:

"If I were damned of body and soul,
I know whose prayers would make me whole,
Mother o' mine, O mother o' mine!"

So God becomes conscious of Himself in various moods of thinking, feeling, and willing in a way in which He could not be conscious but for the individual. And we are therefore no longer to tolerate any philosophy which teaches us to lose any part of the glorious experience of objective consciousness. The objective consciousness is the development of personality and the ability to unfold more finely. Up to the time of the development

of the self-conscious individual God has been expressed only on the plane of mechanical law, with
all the marvels it reveals, in planetary systems, and
growing grass and living things. But these, while
conscious and alive with intelligence, have never had
the ability to plan and choose for themselves. They
have accepted things as they have found them. *We*
do not have to do that. We can take things as they
are and then make them what we want them to be.
We can make plans and start enterprises. We can
distribute the finest emotions of God. We can be
not only conscious of ourselves, but of all other
selves, and finally of that Greater Self which God
is. We can have personal relationships with that
Divine Wonder. To believe, then, that it is desirable to push back into the undifferentiated flow of
life from which we have emerged is to do violence
to the great purpose of Being which is to become
manifest in higher and differentiated forms.

OUR UNITY WITH THE ALL-SELF.

At the same time, the self could not be at all unless it rested back on a common unit, the underly-
ing absolute self; nor could we have any sense of
relationship to these other selves, unless we were
within an all-comprehensive self that relates us.
We must never lose sense of this unity for it is this
that gives our love an all-embracing charity so that
we can look into the faces of the vilest, and below
all the scum or the veneer of life may find our

brother and our sister.   Even the wild creatures of
the plain will become objects of respect and care
for us, because they are included in the one mind
and in their several ways are expressing a purpose
of God.   Thus love and attention to the needs of
animals is a part of every noble man's duty.

Nor shall we, through the use of terms, ever ob-
scure the wholeness of life and the unity of all.
The objective and subjective sides of mind will
then be found to be one; and the former is simply
the outpush of the latter into expression.   Nor
again shall we essay to live by the use of the will,
the rationalizing powers, the inductions of the objective mind alone, but rather learn to lean on the
source and strength of the inner life to which we
are eternally related.

There is, then, no "mortal mind *and* divine mind."
There is but one mind.   The intellectualizing mind
may have chosen wrongly; but it is not another
alien mind.   So to consider is to introduce another
form of dualism.   Sin and evil and sickness are
due to a sense of separation, not to "mortal mind."
They are due to a failure to recognize or employ
the whole power that lies back of us or to partial
knowledge.   In other words, we find that all we
call ill, is due to some form of partialness; and,
when we once more restore the consciousness of
wholeness, we shall do away with the so-called
evil.

Being is always perfect: it is only in becoming

that the apparent imperfection is manifest. Imperfection has its beginning, not in Being or First Cause, but in the mould of thought. As the individual rises into the consciousness of self, with the powers of conscious selection, he may think in either direction, forward or back. Just because he is to enjoy the fun of assembling the parts into the unity, he has within himself the power to combine the factors in the wrong way or to leave some out. When he does that trouble results. Then he will have pain to set him back on the track and push him on again.

Let us therefore constantly keep in mind the essential nature of the One Being and our own relationship to it and have no fear of any issue or problem. We are founded on the Rock of Ages.

Related as we are to the Eternal, All-Powerful, Creative Mind, we must realize that for us to choose is for it to choose, since it has become us for that purpose. Yet because it has given us individuality to choose what we will, it must also make for us or create for us the thing that we choose; or else we would not have any true choice. Then because we choose unwisely or without knowledge of all the factors in the case, let us not despair nor blame God. The only evil is incompleteness. And that is not an evil. For the evil entirely disappears when we learn the whole truth and then employ it.

And this ought to explain to us how there can be the experience of evil and yet no moral fault in God. As Absolute Self, He does not experience evil, because He never has any sense of partialness. His is always a sense of wholeness. *All* the factors are known to Him; and He never thinks in terms of the relative. And so, since God could not be all without sharing every human experience, still the suffering is only in the individual; it is not in God as a consuming experience, for in the Absolute Self there is never any partial choice. God chooses with every factor known. Pain, then, might lie in the order of the eternally possible, or else we could not experience it; yet it never gets hold of God for in Him it is ever transcended by complete knowledge and perfect choice.

CHAPTER VIII.

MAN'S GREATER BODY AND THE FEELING-LIFE.

WE have now shown that the whole round circle of being and its manifestation from star to farthest star and beyond is Mind. Everything originates in Mind; all things are thoughts; all form is idea; all substance is mental. Even what we call spiritual things can be but thought in finer form; and spiritual men and women are those whose thoughts are purest, finest, and most godlike. Love itself is the unified consciousness; and its emotions are the distilled essence of higher thinking. Herein is God made manifest as one, for we cannot conceive of anything apart from Mind; and there is no place outside of that Mind.

Yet for the purposes of clearness, we may have other names for God and other words for that which goes on in Mind. Original Feeling is a name which we may give to First Cause because God becomes manifest through the impulses of feeling-life. This term indicates the depth of thought; it is not merely the idle floating of imagination out into space but the rich conviction of a purpose.

Thus, feeling may be called in general the creative quality in God and so in man. Again, we may note that certain types of thought tend to group themselves to form a particular attribute of mind. Low vibrations of thought become inorganic matter and take form as such. Higher vibrations become cell life and tissues and act harmoniously together as organic laws of physiology and biology.

Finer thought forces assemble themselves around a common center and form what we may call the feeling-body. This is that expression of the self which is distinctly personal but not obvious as is the physical body. As the substance is still thought, the expression is vibration; and as there must be form wherever there is vibration, the "feeling-body" must have form and occupy space in some way. Can we really find the presence of such a feeling-body of each of us; and, if so, what is its extent, nature, and purpose?

Because we are so accustomed to judge our universe from the standpoint of what we can see, touch, and measure with physical instruments, it is hard for us to realize how much of the objective world itself is invisible to us. Yet we are surrounded by innumerable forms of life and "matter" which we cannot cognize by the ordinary senses. Says Flammarion, "Between the last acoustic sensation perceived by our ears and due to 36,850 vibrations per second and the first optical sensation perceived by our eye which is due to four hun-

dred trillion vibrations per second, we perceive
nothing. There is an enormous interval to which
no one of our senses brings us into relation." [1]

We see, then, that forms can and do undoubt-
edly exist around us of which we are not at all
conscious. And, as there are those whose powers
of sight transcend the physical instrument of the
eye, we might expect that such forms would be frequently detected. Such indeed is the case; and
throughout the ages, people who have often been
called clairvoyant, that is, able to see without the
eye, have declared that they could see a more subtle
body surrounding other individuals. This body has
sometimes been called the aura, and has been represented in art by the halo which surrounds the
heads of saints. In the case of Spanish art, it is
usually triangular. In other art, it is oval or represented by the halo about the head. In recent times,
science has made it possible for any one who wishes
to investigate these phenomena to do so, especially
by the use of photographic plates. For it is quite
possible now to photograph the fine vibration or
odic fluid that radiates from all of us. Says Maeterlinck, "Reichenbach was first to discover that
'sensitive' persons could see the effluvia in the dark.
After experiments, he proved that its power varied
with the emotions and status of mind of the sub-
jects. He found that it was of bluish color on
the right side, and yellowish on the left."

---

[1] *The Unknown*, page 11.

The power of this fluid, then, "varies with the emotions and status of mind of the subject." This we would know from the fact that everything has its origin in mind; and that this feeling-body is simply the form in which the higher consciousness of the individual clothes itself. And we may add to this the fact that this feeling-body is also affected profoundly by the thoughts and acts of other people. For example, a very sensitive person was asked by the experimenter to put his hand in a glass of water. He did so and was then removed to another part of the room. A pin was thrust into the water; and he not only was conscious of it but winced with the pain as much as though the pin had been thrust into his physical body.

In another case, a photographic plate was placed within the radiations of the odic fluid emanating from a subject, and scratches were made on the hands in the photograph. The subject at once burst into tears; and the scratches were plainly to be seen on his own hands.[2]

That the feeling-life is not confined to the physical body as we ordinarily see it can be demonstrated in a simpler experiment. Many sensitive persons will show pain if a pin be thrust into the confluence of wave vibrations from the body, at

[2]It is not my purpose here to discuss the question as to how many bodies an individual might have, that is, the different types of vibration; but only to show the extent to which the feeling-life manifests in our experience. Therefore no distinction is attempted between aura, odic fluid, etc.

one-half an inch or an inch-and-a-half beyond the surface.

My purpose, in these illustrations which might easily be extended, is to show a primary fact of mental science, that intelligence, mind, thought, and therefore feeling are not confined to physical organs in the ordinary sense. It is quite possible, indeed, that our future investigations will persuade us that the ego-self functions through still finer instruments than any we have as yet detected and is not at all confined to immediate environment; but for the present this will lead us far enough. We are housed in a wonderful body, very sensitively adjusted to our environment. This body, both *within* the "physical frame" and in the more subtle exterior, is charged with an emotional or feeling consciousness. This consciousness is in general independent of the physical structure and nerve-centers. It uses them; it acts upon them and reacts to them; but still it is independent of them. It is possible to see without eyes and hear without ears, and feel without physical contacts.

Two other characteristics of this feeling-consciousness should be mentioned. First, *it is the medium through which the conscious mind acts upon the physical structure*. It lies, as it were, between the conscious or objective mind and the physical body and environment. Whatever we desire to accomplish on the physical plane must be accom-

plished through it. We give our instructions to it;
and it carries them out.

Second, *the feeling-consciousness is impersonal.*
It does not initiate any movement in the body or
in the thought. It takes any impression given it
and reports it or causes the body to react to it.
If the hand of the subject is scratched on the photographic plate, this consciousness feels it and records
it in the body and in the mind. It varies, as
Maeterlinck has told us, with the emotions and
status of the individual concerned. We thus have
confirmed again that it is simply a form of the
creative activity of mind and is really the mind
functioning impersonally.

THE FEELING-LIFE AFFECTED BY THOUGHT.

We are now ready to see how this intermediary
agent operates in regard to the affairs of our lives
and the very destiny of our souls. We have found
that the feeling-body or consciousness is very sus-
ceptible to mental influence of any kind. It is open
to thought coming from any direction, from either
without or within. These thoughts fall as seed
upon fertile soil; and, as this consciousness has no
will of its own but only an instinct to create, it begins to take any thought and work upon it.
Throughout our lives, seed continues to fall; and
the person who is unconscious of these laws is
always open to unseen and unknown influences from
without. How quickly we catch the contagion of

fear around us! How strangely we react to another's mood. How open we are to impressions;
and how often we are swept off the feet of our
better judgment by some strong mind! How frequently we become downcast without apparent
cause and then rise to an unexpected buoyancy of
spirit! Some one says, "You do not look well;"
and at once we begin to feel our pulse. Another
says, "Times are going to be hard;" and we begin
to feel the pinch of those times. Worst of all, we
are all open to vagrant thoughts and ideas which
are always flying about, for a thought is a vibration
and goes on its frictionless way through the ethers.
These thoughts, as though they were angels, come
to the heart that is like them; or, like devils, they
flock to the place where they feel most at home.
Thus the sins of our fathers are visited upon us,
if we let them visit—and most of us keep a spare
chamber. Especially are we open to the invasion
of thoughts directed purposely at us. There are
those who envy and those who oppose our plans
and purposes. Often they do not consciously wish
us harm; but they are thinking such thoughts about
us as are not for our best good. If we are unguarded, these thoughts come to us, find entrance
through the impersonal, neutral consciousness and
make their impression upon it. Being impersonal
and creative, this consciousness registers on our
bodies as disease; on our conditions, as failure;
on our minds, as depression. So if one were really

hostile to us, he might deliberately practice "black magic," which is by no means out of fashion. In that case, his thought would gather up all the forces of negative thought which were not consciously directed at us; and one hostile mind could then lead an army of inimical forces against us.

PROTECTION AGAINST MALICIOUS SUGGESTION BY CONSCIOUS THOUGHT.

On the other hand, our protection is quite adequate. We must remember that no physical or mental reaction is possible except through the consciousness. If, then, we *allow* hostile impressions or suggestions to be made upon it, then disaster will follow. If, on the other hand, we insist that no influence shall affect us except by our own conscious choice, then the consciousness will not pick up the flying thought. We are like the wireless telegraph instrument, we record only those messages to which our instrument is attuned. A full protection is thus assured against the most malicious influence by the simple expedient of declaring that you will not receive such thoughts from any direction. It is even a good plan in some cases to ridicule the power of such thoughts in cases where you feel that mental pressure is being brought to bear upon you. Judge Troward says, "Look it mentally in the face and say, 'Cock-a-doodle-doo!'" And that is not bad advice. Every one should occasionally think of himself as surrounded by an impenetrable barrier which no negative thought can enter. We are moving through a world more subtle than we have supposed; and we may as well cognize the unseen forces of evil long enough—and no longer—to declare our protection against them. "No evil shall befall me, because I have made the Most High my habitation."

We are frequently in the presence of strong-minded people who without meaning to use bad mental influences, still desire us to do their will or accept their dictum. They not only cause their thought to impinge on our sensitive consciousness to act as suggestion; but a real force goes out from them. The odic fluid of which we have previously spoken is a subtle form of force which probably emanates from large numbers of individuals and strikes directly upon the organism unless we protect ourselves. This force can be photographed. It is strong enough to cause a lever to tip, a copper needle to vibrate, or to set a clock in motion within a sealed glass vessel. It is powerful enough to move a table weighing two hundred pounds, and to magnetize minerals. Many healers send it forth in the treatment of patients, usually draining their own forces in using it. I have treated healers who felt this influence go forth from them in waves. I have known of others who in healing send off this current in an encircling motion, going out to the patient and returning again.

One can imagine with what energy such a force

impinges directly upon the organism of those toward whom it is directed. This probably explains those cases of remarkable personal magnetism with which history deals, Julius Cæsar, Napoleon, Washington, and many of our great pioneers. Whole atmospheres are charged with this psychic energy; and places are affected by the presence of one powerful individual.

It seems to me, therefore, that one should occasionally examine his own consciousness to see how much it is affected by the opinions, prejudices, will, and oppositions of others, and counteract any such influences by the quiet direction of his own forces. In the case of cancer and some other diseases, advanced physicians to-day are using powerful electric waves to drive back the vibrations which stream in vivid colors from the affected organ. Shall we do less in protecting ourselves against those attacks of personal magnetism which, either consciously or unconsciously, are directed against us? And if we can do it in no other way, we should certainly avoid contact with those whose dominating mind overpowers our own will and causes us to move about as puppets at the bid and call of their desires. This is particularly true in the case of those who claim to be the directors of our religious destiny and to know the only way by which our souls can climb into heaven. The religious say-so, the "only-my-way-to-heaven" doctrine is but another way to beat down and imprison the splendid freedom of the soul. So anywhere and everywhere that men would enslave us we must rise up and declare the immortal heritage of our birth, *our will to will our own good.* "Sir," we may say, "I prefer my hell to your heaven, if the choice is not to be my own." Let no man enslave your soul! Thus does each one of us choose the pathway of his destiny.

.   .   .   .   .   ◙

CHAPTER IX.

THE EMOTIONAL SELF AND THE CAUSES OF DISEASE.

WE have seen that the body which we call physical is only a part of man's organism. There is around and within each one of us an area of vibration which is definitely associated with the body, which transmits and receives influences, not by physical contacts alone but also by the more subtle agency of thought and feeling. This greater body has form because it is definite enough to occupy space; and yet the form is doubtless continuously changing and altering. The whole organism, which includes this, is conscious, that is, it has intelligence, is open to the impressions which are constantly being made upon it, and faithfully reports them to the self. At the same time, we must remember that this consciousness is the impersonal activity of mind; it does not think as "I," the ego, think; it does not have ideas. *It takes them.* It takes them from me; or it takes them from without, *unless I tell it not to.* It is thus a great blessing or a great curse to man that he has this neutral field of consciousness. If he controls the images that it receives, if he consciously directs his life, if he prohibits the invasion of false thoughts and suggestions he has reason to be grateful for the neutral activity of mind, for it is his silent partner, his willing worker who takes his orders and continues to build the body and to care for the whole organism without any great amount of thought on the part of the conscious self. If, on the other hand, you and I are ignorant or careless of the influences which surround and affect us, we are continuously open to the invasion of disease, unhappiness, poverty and all the brood of negative thought-devils. For the neutral consciousness takes the impression that is given to it and passes it on as the working model of the cell-life; and each cell takes the architect's plans and begins to build accordingly. This is the way in which contagious diseases get their innings. The individual is not always consciously thinking of or fearing the disease; but his consciousness is open to the inroads of any thought that may come blowing along on the winds of fate. For him who lives by conscious choices, life is therefore destiny; for him who lives by chance, life is fate.

All persons vary in the degree with which the creative or feeling consciousness is affected by ideas and influences. Some people are very sensitive and are open to the slightest impression. To be sensitive is simply to leave the field of the feeling-consciousness unguarded and to allow others to sow the fatal seeds of their thoughts and opinions upon the rich soil within. Then we experience it as pain; or, as we often say, "My feelings are hurt." And as each emotion seeks an outlet at the weakest point, these feelings make their impress upon the flesh in all forms of disorder.

Diseases in women can be largely traced to the reactions of the emotional life. From the fact that their love nature is more tender and gentle than that of men, and that they do not have the excitement of continuous change in the work of the day which falls to the lot of the average workingman, women allow the inharmony of things to make a deeper impression upon them. Any thought brooded upon holds it in consciousness; and, as creative mind and its physical agent continue to act upon each thought so long as it is held, the result is often fatal to happiness and health. Thus even words that are not meant to contain a sting are held to the bosom like the poisonous asp until peace and love are stung to death. The husband goes to his work and forgets his hasty words before nightfall calls him again to his home; but the wife does not forget. The thought goes on rankling in her breast until its inevitable end in some form of nervous or physical disorder. Says Edward Rowland Sill:

"These clumsy feet still in the mire
  Go crushing blossoms without end:
These hard, well-meaning hands we thrust
  Among the heart-strings of a friend.

> The ill-timed truth we might have kept—
> Who knows how sharp it pierced and stung!
> The word we had not sense to say,
> Who knows how grandly it had rung!"

Sometimes I think that unintentional hurts are more cruel than those that are given in some burst of anger because to be thoughtless along some lines is an indication that we have not cared enough to think how it will affect the other. Then the other cannot but feel that we have not been true to love; and nothing hurts like neglect. Without love there is nothing; and love languishes on neglect and thoughtlessness. A white-hot iron across the breast will not so mar the body as the word and act that burns its way into the soul of those who had reason to expect better.

Few men or women would think of plunging a dagger into another's flesh; and yet they use the tongue which is a two-edged sword and turn it within the wound. It pierces the vital atmosphere of the emotional life and makes its mark upon the creative consciousness within. Thus both soul and body are plunged into hell.

The day will come when we shall put a heavy fine upon the man or woman who predicts disaster and disease, and utters croaking forecasts of coming evil, for he is cursing the race. Yet to-day we turn the pages of our newspapers and read of those who prognosticate the return of some dreadful scourge, or some great cataclysm of nature, and then lay out the tools of their industry ready to reap the harvest which their foul seed has caused to spring up. Direful forecasts, pratings of so-called evil times, fault-finding, pessimistic utterances, slander, gossip of a malicious character—all these are the spawn and the incubus of disease, want and misery, for they fall on the fertile and productive soil of the race-consciousness and, entering any door that swings upon unsuspecting hinges, they make their abode within the body. Here, like a serpent, they coil for the spring, like its bite, they fester in the flesh. Whole peoples have been extinguished by the false gods of the national ideals and ideas, for "thought is father to the act;" and ideas, making their impress upon the creative mind of the individual, the race, and the cosmic consciousness alike bring forth the dread cancer that burns out the life of the nation.

OUR TENDENCY TO YIELD TO SUGGESTIONS OF DISASTER.

How invidious are the temptations of our life when the very individual who reads this may exclaim, "Yes, that is so. See what I have suffered from the tongue and acts of others. They have brought it upon me!" This is perhaps a natural thought but a very dangerous one, for if it be true that we must *accept* these things we are bound to the chariot wheel of the most vulgar thinker among us. This is incredible. We are children of choice.

We are rulers of this organism by right of that divine freedom within us which determines what thoughts and impressions shall be admitted to consciousness. The conscious self is the gatekeeper in the house of the lord of our life and can challenge all comers. "Who are you? What is your purpose? Do you bode ill or good? Do you seek to enslave me or to serve me?"

For we must realize that the feeling-life is not objective but subjective. It is that which we discern as the greater body of the individual and is primarily controlled by his mind. While, therefore, we are to guard against unconscious control of our lives and fate from without, we are not to lose sight of the fact that we of ourselves are constantly initiating the causes which bring disease and unhappiness upon us.

EMOTIONS THAT POISON.

That intense emotions do create physical reactions with startling suddenness is shown in the case of those investigations which have been made in examining the blood of people under the stress of excitement of one kind or another. It is found that the normal secretions of the body do not take place but in their stead frequently some kind of poison is distilled by the overwrought cells and glands. Fear, anger, jealousy, hate, and so on, each produce some form of substance poisonous to the system. A mother in fear or hate has been

known to poison the milk of her babe. Under
stress of worry, the stomach will often turn the
gastric juice to acid. An extreme of the reaction
of feeling upon the physical organs came to my
attention in the case of a woman who lost her sight
because she vehemently declared that she wished
she might never see her husband's face again. She
was afterwards healed through the science of
mind.

Cases of quite frequent occurrence have been
recorded during the centuries wherein religious
zealots through strong feeling have re-lived the life
and suffering of Jesus to the extent that they have
caused the mars and scars of his hands, feet and
side, to be reproduced on their own.

THE PAINS OF LOVE.

Love that is unrequited or that is constantly vio-
lated in its finer instincts has a power of reacting
on the system with terrible force. A sort of stifling
takes place throughout the whole body. Shrinking
of the nerve cells, and a kind of congestion is felt;
and a "soul-sickness" lays hold of one. When love
is hurt, feeling itself seems ready to die; and the
whole body and mind is plunged into a distraught
condition. The heart cries out against it, and
against the fate which love, more cruel than hate,
has prepared for the tortured soul. Here is where
the ministry of truth alone can soothe the broken
heart and restore lost confidence and hope. It is

a vast issue, for life is pitted against death, and faith against bitter loss.

At first one should seek some change of interest. Anything that will alter the thought life should be sought. Service to others in hard straits of life will often beguile a mind fastened on sorrow. Sympathy for those who need our help will do much. But for those who know the law more vigorous measures are also desirable. One may as well face the fact at once. There is nothing comes to us but something in us brings it. We may not have consciously brought it; but here it is. Is the one from whom we have received the all but mortal hurt really our mate? If not, then it is best that things should end between us. If so, then time or tide cannot keep us forever apart. The boundless reaches of time are vast enough to work out every plan and purpose; and no heart but sometime will find its life complete. Firmly recognize that only ourselves keep our good from us and only ourselves draw our good to us; and we are ready to act. Then boldly lay claim on the law for the best that life can give. When the perfect concept is formulated, hold to it throughout every vicissitude of changing times and at last the power of creative thought through conscious choice will draw to us love's best though now it seems to lie beyond the grave.[1]

Some day the clouds shall lift
And I shall see God's face there in the rift.

[1] For the healing power of love, see Chapter XVII.

PSYCHIC DISEASE.

We have thus seen that what we frequently call the psychic nature opens us to the invasion of health or disease, for the same feeling-life that takes the imprint and contagion of disease is also open to the contagion of good health and well-being. In our practice as healers, too, we shall frequently discover that the patient is not suffering from the actual presence of physical disorders as in the case of cancer, tuberculosis, anemia, and so on, but is suffering from what is as yet only the psychic counterpart. In other words, the feeling-life is distressed; and the organ that is affected is only vibrating to the inharmony of the consciousness resident within it. In such cases, we can often effect an immediate cure through the removal of the thought cause. This would be an instantaneous cure. Where the physical organ has become diseased or deformed, a slower reaction often occurs. This, however, is not so much due to the difficulty of changing the physical tissues as in changing the thought or consciousness of the sufferer. The cell-life is stamped with the image of disease, and we must restore the perfect concept before the physical change takes place. I have known of instantaneous cures taking place so rapidly that growths have slipped away bodily, or swellings have been reduced so quickly as to cause a great itching and momentary heat. In such case, the emotional life or consciousness was immediately affected. This frequently happens with children especially, because they take the word of the healer on perfect trust, and as faith is everything, verily it has its own reward.

We are having some remarkable instances of the physical effect of emotional experiences in these days, on account of the abnormal psychology of the battle-field. The close relation between mind and body is continually being illustrated. Take the case of men who through shell-shock or fear have lost sight and hearing. In some instances, these same men have had sight and hearing restored by a counter fear. For example when the hospital-ship which was bringing them home was sunk, the need for sight or hearing in order to protect them from the new peril was so great as to stimulate the creative activity so that they were able once more to use their eyes and ears. Fear acts in such cases as a strong image of desire, the impact of thought is insistent; and the needed power of the organ is instantaneously restored.

Mental science has not found it necessary to make any wide discrimination between what is called functional and organic disease because the same power controls both and heals both. Disease is simply the image of wrong-thinking sustained in consciousness until the deformed creation takes place. Health is the right image acted upon in the same way. It is probable, however, that a correct diagnosis will help materially in case patient and healer do not have a high state of consciousness or faith. In that case the error of thought is successfully combated by higher knowledge; fear is removed by a better understanding; and the true concept of health is restored to the mind and the afflicted organ. This is certainly true in psychoanalytic practice. At the same time, we need never stand abashed in the presence of any disease, be it purely psychic or not. Spirit is all from one end of the scale to the other; and faith and persistency will heal. All disease is mental since all is mind; and organic troubles are simply the deeper-seated habit of wrong concepts. Disease and health are alike mental habits.

THE EMOTIONS OF HEALTH AND HAPPINESS.

It thus becomes clear to us that the emotional or creative life is profoundly affected by our thought and, being entirely neutral, goes on functioning in the flesh according to the dominant idea. It is just as true for health and happiness as it is for the reverse. And as the majority of men think healthful and hopeful thoughts, we find more well people than sick ones, although almost every one at some time or another opens himself to the invasion of wrong thinking. Pride of achievement, ambition, love, hope, faith, a general desire for decency—these and many other qualities keep the mind of the race largely occupied and are guarantees against the false ideas and ideals of a lower order of living. Whatever most fills the mind will most govern the destiny whether it be high or low, good or bad. We make our way through the world, we build our hell or heaven, we crawl or soar, we sink or swim by the choice of the thoughts that daily swarm in the throne-room of the mind. There within sits the Christ-self, master of life and happiness. He alone passes final decree. His word is law. The feeling-life, the creative intelligence within, is his servant doing whatsoever his will shall desire. Infinite in resources because heir of the ages and one with the Eternal; possessing powers transcendent and able to choose what he will have, man passes through the world, selecting what pathway of destiny he shall follow, what mountains he shall climb, to what stars his soul shall soar, through the selection of those things that fill his mind and thus direct his creative consciousness.

CHAPTER X.

CHOOSING WHAT WE WANT.

WE have now seen that we live in the One Mind which thinks what it wants and puts forth into expression what it thinks. The substance of the universe is intelligence or life on the invisible side and the various forms are ideas. On the visible side of nature, substance and form are vibration or energy. But ideas are expressed in the form of thought; and thought is also energy, so that the visible universe is God's thought. We found, too, that Being thinks definite thoughts or chooses what it wants. In this way, it acts in a personal capacity. Then its Creative Activity comes into play and makes what it chooses come forth into form. In this way, it acts impersonally. Being cannot be impersonal, but it can act impersonally. By the courtesy of words, we may often speak of Being or Mind as impersonal, as referring to its impersonal activity. Yet we shall lose the very sweetness of life if we do not recognize this fact: as Personal Spirit, God loves, feels, wills, using the terms in the philosophical sense. God does not love, feel, or will always exactly in the human way, except through the individual. As the Absolute Person, He cannot love, feel, or will in any way that would deny His absoluteness or wholeness of vision. As impersonal law, He creates whatever idea is selected either by Him or another for creation.

If, now, we•will liken the Divine Creative Mind in its impersonal capacity to the soil, we shall have a good picture of the way the impersonal mind works for us. In fact, the soil *is* the Universal Creative Mind in one of its aspects, for it is the impersonal mind functioning in vibration. Now we all know that the soil has no personal will, or purpose of its own. It is entirely impersonal or neutral. It does not care whether God scatters the seed as He may have done at the beginning of the visible creation, or whether the tree scatters it, or you or I. It will take your seed as quickly as it will take mine. Again, it does not care whether the seed given to it is one kind or another. It does not, as impersonal mind, care what seed is given it. It takes all seeds into its bosom with equal love and care, and begins to grow each thing after its kind.

That which we call our subjective mind is one with the universal impersonal mind, so that whatever seed of thought or idea we scatter in our mind will take root there and grow impersonally. Whatever thought is most strongly impressed upon this mind will take the deepest root. That is why some people are never sick. No thought of sickness has ever deeply impressed itself upon their mind and so the creative activity within has gone on normally, continuously building a healthy body. There is only a sense of well-being; and spirit accordingly passes through into manifestation in perfect expression. It is a hard saying but true that we only have to *feel* well to be well. Accordingly every effort must be made to bring the feeling-life to the point of quietness and ease, that the perfect work of healing may go on, since the feeling-life and the creative are one.

USING THE UNIVERSAL IMPERSONAL MIND.

Now whatever is true of the individual impersonal mind in the way of choice is also true of the universal. For as there is in reality no point of demarcation between the *being* which man is and the *Being* which spirit *is*, so *there is no point at which the inner mind fails to contact the mind of the infinite. Both minds act alike; they produce according to the kind and strength of the thought or idea impressed upon them.*

On one point, however, we should exercise care. We should never suppose that Being will act in any way contrary to the law of its own nature. For example, no amount of suggestion from us will ever cause it to make water run uphill, or repeal the law of the attraction of gravitation, or set the sun back half an hour. Having once chosen a *way* of acting, this way is its law and Being goes on to create in accordance with it. (See Chapter XIV, page 115.) Yet this need never interfere with our hopes and plans, for there is room for everything we can desire within the scope of the law; and each one of these laws can be made our servant. Conforming ourselves to the law, we can harness the water; we can depend upon the stability of things that come through the attraction of the earth; and we can employ the rays of the sun to grow our gardens and to light our path. And each law is thus transcended by adapting ourselves to it, as in the case of flying, for example. Nor is it inconceivable that man shall learn how to avoid the pull of attraction through higher knowledge; we may yet fly without anything more than a good pair of closet wings; and a new Ford may rise to speed us over the pathway of the skies.

But with this warning and encouragement, let us see how we may legitimately hope to employ the impersonal forces of the one and only mind in which we find ourselves. Through recognition of this unity, we may not only demonstrate over physical conditions of the body; but also, recognizing that things are alive with intelligence, we may learn how to govern them by the higher activity of our own. Thus we may demonstrate or realize prosperity, or the reverse, for poverty comes in the same way. The Greater Mind, being impersonal and creative, and acting upon the image or impress of prosperity or poverty, of joy or sorrow, as the case may be, produces "according to our faith."

Impersonal Mind a Magic Mirror.

The great creative mind is like a mirror. It will reflect back to us created just what we face it with. Some of us would be very glad if the glass would reflect back a more flattering face than the one we give it. With an ordinary mirror, this is impossible. With the Cosmic it is the same; but, in the case of the Cosmic, we may give it a fairer idea of what we want. In other words, we can conceive the perfect plan; and it will body it forth in living flesh and tissue. This would be literally true even of our faces. I have known of people using this law to beautify the countenance. I said so to a class at one time and declared that while this was not a beauty parlor, yet it could do the work of one. I said, "Any one can use the law and become beautiful." One woman raised her hand. "How long would it take?" she asked. I looked at her—and did not answer! I did not know. Nevertheless this should not be considered merely a joke. Whatever concept of the beautiful you may have will ultimately be bodied forth in the face and form if you so decree. Every face is a reflex of the thought-life behind it; and a good psychologist can get a very straight idea of the thought-life by even a casual glance at the features in which it is registered. Our bodies are the aggre-

gate of our thinking passed into form. "Whatsoever a man soweth that shall he also reap." You
cannot sow onion seeds and reap a bouquet of sweet
peas. "Neither do men gather figs of thorns, nor
grapes of thistles," said Jesus, who knew. "According to your faith, be it unto you," he said.
Faith is an attitude of mind; it is the image of
expectancy you assume toward the law. According to its kind, the law gives back to you. If you
expect to be cheated, you will be cheated. If you
expect honesty, you will find it. The man who
runs around with a chip on his shoulder will meet
an Irishman on every corner. We get in this
world a return in kind. Says Lytton,

> "Let any man once show the world that he feels
> Afraid of its bark, and 'twill fly at his heels;
> Let him fearlessly face it, 'twill leave him alone
> But 'twill fawn at his feet if he flings it a bone."

It is on this basis that our destiny is determined
by our attitudes of mind. He who faces the world
with good cheer and a smile, will see the world
smile back; but he who faces it with a grouch will
hear its growl. The law is inexorable. Sooner or
later, it pays us back in kind—"an eye for an eye
and a tooth for a tooth." Of it Jesus said, "Not
one jot or one tittle shall pass away until all be
fulfilled." In even the smallest matters, it works
with precision. What seeds of discord some are
now sowing. "Sowing to the wind they reap the
whirlwind!" How many are cursing themselves and

others. We hear some say on rising, "I suppose I will lose money to-day." "I fear ruin for my business." "Probably the rheumatism will bother me to-day again. It's damp." "I expect people won't understand me if I do this, even if it is right." And the "thing we greatly fear comes upon us." Why? Because we attract it! We have already damned ourselves by expecting it. That was our "word" to the law; and it becomes flesh and dwells among us.

Our "word" is our image or the seed we sow. If we sow words and thoughts of inharmony, we must reap discord. As Jesus said in explaining the parable, "The seed is the word." It falls into the soil—or divine creative mind—and it "grows we know not how." How choice then must we be of our words! The Master Metaphysician said, "By thy words thou shalt be justified and by thy words thou shalt be condemned." We must *choose* wisely our words or attitudes of mind. We are told by the poet:

> Give love and love to your life will flow,
> A strength in your utmost need;
> Have faith, and a thousand hearts will show
> Their faith in your word and deed.
>
> For life is the mirror of king and slave,
> 'Tis just what you are and do;
> Then give to the world the best you have
> And the best will come back to you.

The Law is a mirror. Choose wisely the image of thought you give to it!

CHAPTER XI.

PICTURING OUR GOOD.

IT is because of the infinite and accurate responsiveness of law that we are told by all metaphysicians the value of forming our concept or image of reality. Many teachers tell us to visualize or mentally picture the thing we desire. But it is not so much a necessity to form the image as it is to have the expectancy. The inner mind of us will often mold the pattern, for "there is a Spirit in man and the inspiration of the Almighty gives him understanding." The major necessity is really not so much to picture the thing, as it is to present the idea to the creative mind. "Before they call, I will answer them.—For the Father knoweth what things ye have need of, before ye ask them." On many occasions I have made demonstrations in prosperity where the result seemed quite different from the anticipation—but better. Why was this? It was because in all honesty we were seeking the best. We did not know the absolute best; but creative mind did. We presented to creative mind the idea we wanted worked out according to the best pattern we could make. And as the artist sketches the idea which he wishes to embody in a picture, and then paints it with a skill beyond his first vision, so the Master Architect, the Law, paints for us, or brings into objective manifestation for us the idea which we held up as the "image" or "word" to it. This explains many cases where the spirit of healer and patient is right, even though their concept or image is apparently faulty. The great creative mind reflects back to us our coveted good—with its universal plus added to it. Just as Jesus said of those who give generously, "Give and it shall be given unto you, good measure pressed down and running over shall men give into your bosom."

HOW TO USE THE IMAGINATION FOR CREATION.

It now becomes necessary to make even clearer the principle of ideation of which we have been speaking. We must learn to distinguish the activity of creative law through ideation as opposed to concentration. We must learn the infinite superiority of the one over the other, if we are to become successful in the work of healing and helping humanity. It is through the principle of ideation or image formation that the Spirit creates or passes itself into manifestation. Being is becoming manifest through the creative faculty acting on the pure image which Spirit projects. When Spirit begins to create a universe, it has at first no pattern by which to guide its creation. It has no rose uttering its sweetness on the air; no bird a-twitter in its leafy nest; no star gleaming in the crystal blue. It cannot have these as a pattern for they do not exist as yet. It must therefore use its imagination; it must imagine a rose; it must picture a star. And so it does. In the vast chamber of Originating Spirit, the divine canvas is unrolled; and the Great Artist dreams forth the beauty of the spheres. Celestial visionings! Glorified concepts! Spirit sketching-in a world! But whatever God Thinks must become. Being at once begins its becoming; and the great Law of Mind, which is its method of activity, takes up the image and bodies forth a world. This is the meaning of Genesis, "The Spirit of God moved upon the waters." "Waters" is the esoteric term for the Law, or Creative Mind. The divine idea impresses itself on the Creative Mind; and a world passes out of spirit into manifestation.

Man repeats the creative process. As spirit acts, so he. He dreams a dream, and the creative forces body it forth. He says, "Let this thing be;" and it becomes. He does not make it; he accepts it. See how it is all lifted out of the region of struggle! He does not have to say his beads, nor "do" his affirmations, nor concentrate desperately upon it. We have had people enter our office, with their will "all screwed up to the sticking point," muscles tense, teeth set, determined to see the thing through. —If will can work, it surely will! They have got hold of a thought and are clinging to it like grim death.

NOT WILL BUT FAITH.

This form of concentration is to say the least, unwise, whether practiced on oneself or another. It acts on the supposition that the mind or will of the individual is creating something rather than controlling its creation. Indeed the will does have some power; but the minute the thought is diverted, everything flies apart. Many become discouraged after practicing this method for a time. Their thoughts fly away from them; and they despair of ever catching them again. They find a "good thought," corner it, grab it by a wing—and it slips out of their hands! Away it goes; and they after it over the fence and through a hundred back-yards! Finally it is again captured but only to escape, until the wearied mind gives up the pursuit and says, "I haven't will enough to do it." Yet healing on this basis, that of the human will rather than the Divine Mind, has been the only kind generally accepted by organized religion. This fact is easily proven by reference to literature on the subject. The world has been slow to learn the lesson the Master taught: "Take my yoke—the yoke of the Spirit—upon you, and learn of me;—for my yoke is easy and my burden is light." The way of the Spirit is a better way. Concentration is not your curative agent! "Of mine own self, I can do nothing." The creative mind within you, and the creative mind in which you live, move and have your being, does your work for you. Your part is to formulate your idea and let the Law do the rest. Suppose your mind does wander. If you have formed a clear image of your desire and turned it over to the law, and really believe the law is working on it, and that you will get results, your work is done. "Commit thy ways unto the Lord (or Law), trust also in Him; and He shall bring it to pass." I have healed patients while they were telling me their troubles over the telephone or passing out of a crowded room after a lecture. How? Simply by believing the words of the Master. "Ye shall know the Truth; and the Truth shall set you free. And as the Father hath inherent life in himself, so hath he given it to the son to have inherent life in himself." "The Truth" is the law of spirit's activity. Know that the creative mind is on your job; and "it shall be done unto you, even as ye will."

CONCENTRATION VS. IDEATION.

The difference between the method of "concentration" as an effort of will and "ideation" is that in the former you feel you have something to do; in the latter you have something to be. For, the moment you realize a thing to be true already in Spirit, that moment it is. "Before they call, I will answer them." This, too, is the meaning of the Great Teacher, "When ye pray, believe ye have received; and ye shall receive." Believe that the creative mind has taken up your case, believe that in the absolute of being your desire is already realized, believe that the perfect image or immaculate conception of your mind has registered on the Divine Mind, believe that the spiritual reality or prototype now is, believe that if your vision were keen enough you could now see the health of the body or wealth of estate you crave. If it is a house, that house now is, either on an objective plane or in the finer ether, soon to manifest. "Hast thou faith: only believe," these are the words of the Teacher. Then because ye believe that your good is yours, and that spirit has set it aside for you already, "ye shall receive." Your good is on the way! Being is becoming! Spirit is passing through!

And now some one could object, I suppose, to all this on the ground that it thrusts too much responsibility upon the individual. Are we not in danger of making wrong choices and thus causing the law to operate continuously upon our misshapen images? Will we not constantly be setting forces in motion which we cannot control and thus bring upon ourselves the very evils which we would avoid? And one must answer, "Yes," though I would not admit it as a flaw in the divine order. It is the very token of the sublimity of my own soul that I can choose even hell if I want to. If heaven is to be thrust upon me, who is to thrust it? Your kind of heaven might be hell for me. A certain minister said that it would be heaven for him to recline on a couch through all eternity and have his wife ruffle his hair. "But," he added, "it would be hell for her." And so it might. No, I must be able to choose; and it is no choice at all unless I can choose that which may not be at all for my best good but rather for my worst.

It must be remembered that choice consists in selecting for ourselves those combinations of things and ideas which fit our own particular interest. If we were without choice, we would also be without individuality. Your individuality is different from mine in just this respect, that you select a different set of interests from mine. You prefer a different type of friend; you enjoy games that I do not enjoy; you read different books; you select cake instead of cookies; and you would not perhaps think it fun to bathe in the ocean in winter. The things that interest each of us constitute a set of ideas that are individual. Even were we to eat the same food, breathe the same air, and drink from the same well, we would not be alike. If Jack Spratt and his wife had both eaten fat and both eaten lean, Jack might have been fat while Mrs. Spratt remained lean all of her life, because he thought big jolly thoughts while she worried about everything. She might have been a very thin thinker.

So, of course, we may make mistakes in the selection of our interests and the combination of our ideas. In which case we would get into trouble, for fear and faith amount to the same thing in the end, in that each is an attitude of mind, an idea which will bring to us manifest, just what we have uttered into Creative Mind. The one we call evil, because we do not like it; the other we call good because we do.

But if we bring upon ourselves some deplorable evil, what then? Why it comes; and we do not like it; and we change our way of thinking. Expectancy and wrong choice brought it. Expectancy and changed choice will remove it.

Theory of Denials.

Just here we may well consider the theory of denials which play so much a part in the teaching of some systems of thought. The theory is builded upon the obvious fact that there is something in experience which we do not like, which we call evil. But as God is the All-Good, and there cannot be anything outside of Him, then there cannot be any real evil. It is only apparent. It is an illusion of the mortal mind.

What is wrong in this argument? We have already seen that there can be only one mind and to admit of any other mind that can experience anything at all, is to admit a dual universe, even if we go way round the bush and call it "mortal" or

"human," "carnal," erroneous thought, cinema picture, illusion, lie, and all those other synonyms for
a second mind. And to say that the evil itself is
an illusion, is to say that we can experience an
illusion. In fact, to deny a thing is to confess it,
for if we did not experience it, we would not know
anything about it. But if we can experience an
illusion of pain and evil, is that not just the same
thing as saying that we experience the pain and
evil? "A rose by any other name would smell as
sweet;" and evil by the name of illusion feels as
bad.

We have already seen, however, that whatever
we experience is the physical expression of a super-
physical idea; that is, we bring forth in form just
what we conceive in thought. Our partial view of
things, our mistaken choices, have brought forth
the monstrosity at which we shudder. Clothed in
flesh, we perceive how wrong or vile was our
thought. But here it is in flesh or in circumstance!
What are we to do? Forget what we do not want
and declare what we do want.

In cases where the thought cannot conceive the
perfectly rounded idea of health or prosperity on
account of the immediate circumstances of pain
or lack, it may sometimes help to state, "I do no
longer allow it. It shall not be." In this you do
not deny the experience; but you refuse any longer
to recognize it. I have a great friend, a powerful
healer, who tells me how she acted in her own case.

Being resolved to be free of her sickness, she felt impelled to a vocal declaration, but lived in an apartment where she could not make all the noise she wanted to. So she cast herself on the bed, buried her face in the pillow, drew another over her to stifle the sound and yelled at the top of her lungs, somewhat like this, "I won't be sick. I won't be sick. I will not have it." These may not have been her exact words; but it was her thought; and it healed her.

The purpose is to get rid of the *feeling* one has of suffering and sorrow and unhappiness and want, and make way for the influx of health and all other forms of good. This enables us to hold up the clear image or feeling of the thing we desire, and Creative Mind then has a clear pattern to work upon to bring forth our idea into physical expression.

Thus we see that in this system of teaching there is no room for denials at all.[1]

For to state that we will not be sick or unhappy is really an affirmation. To say that we will not yield to the fear or danger in which we find ourselves is not to deny that what is so plainly evident to us is an experience, but to affirm that it cannot "get us." So the Ninety-First Psalm does not state that no one ever falls or suffers from plague, but it does say, "It shall not come nigh

[1] See also pages 66-68, *How to Develop Faith That Heals*, by the author.

thee. Only with thine eyes [not in your own personal experience] shalt thou behold and see the reward of the wicked. Because he hath set his love upon me, therefore will I deliver him." Deliver him from what? Certainly not from an illusion, but a real peril. "I will set him on high because he hath known my name."

It thus becomes clear that the determining factor of our lives, whether for good or ill, is the concept or idea which we hold. If our thought is ever upward in expectancy, we shall ever draw to us the finest and the best. If we picture the lovely and true, and expect it, verily our faith shall have its reward.

Note what we have said: "If we select our good, and *paint it in living colors of faith, it will come to us."* Many there are who think good thoughts and *wish* for the best to happen. Once in a while there rises a man who commands it to appear; and it does appear because he believes that it will come.

CHAPTER XII.

A DEFINITE METHOD FOR REALIZATION.

WE now see clearly enough that we live in the midst of an All-Embracing Mind which presses in upon us at every point in the unseen nature of intelligence, and everywhere manifests in the forms of loveliness and beauty, in the stupendous and awe-inspiring forces of the earthquake and the storm. For God is God of all and nothing can go on in the great cosmic unfoldments apart from His will. He it was who set the universes afloat in the vast sea of space; and He it is who drives three hundred thousand suns through the measureless race-courses of the universe. There could not be an objective world of stupendous and changing forces without the great cataclysms of nature.

Yet man is to fear nothing in the midst of them, for he can mount on the wings of spiritual understanding; he can walk upon the waves of a changing world; he can pass unscathed through the torrent and the flame; he can escape from every peril, through the mastership of his spirit. He *can* if he *will but choose.* He must choose to depend upon the higher intuitions of his soul to guide his steps, and the genius of his own mind to select that good which he desires to manifest for him.

We see, therefore, that it is of the utmost importance for us to understand that we live in a world of law; that substance is mind, and that the determining factor is choice. God's choices are the great cosmic ones; He does not interfere with ours. In other words, God sets in motion great laws by which the world and man is evolved. He makes selection of definite lines of activity and then goes on unfolding along those lines to the ultimate conclusion. So regular is the operation of his mind in these great operations that we may well call it law, and depend upon it that it cannot be broken. Jesus, the Master Teacher of the Law of Mind, said, "Not one jot nor one tittle shall be taken away from the law, until all be fulfilled." In other words, the law is absolutely exact, and can be depended upon to produce each thing after its kind of thought.

The first step for us to take is to put the mind in an attitude of expectant faith.[1]

We can make statements of our attitude, for they inspire our confidence. They hold the mind steady. They keep the image or idea clear. They assert our faith. As a man whistles to inspire his own cheer, so we say to ourselves, "Cheer up, it's

---

[1]See Lesson III, "How to Use the Law—the Silence," in *The Law of Mind in Action*, by the author.

all coming out all right." "Cheer up," said Jesus, "thy *faith* hath saved thee, go in peace." Statements of truth are always helpful in inspiring our confidence and expectancy, unless we turn them into magic formulas and phrases, when they lose most of their power. Words are designed to produce a corresponding *feeling* on the inner plane; if they fail to do this, they have no value. In so far as they succeed in doing this, however, they have creative value. It is because words almost invariably engender *feeling* that we are to guard against their idle use. The purpose of statements is to lead us into *realization* of the truth that is to make us free.

We must rid the mind of any sense of struggle, for if we plant the seed the soil will do all the work for us. "The seed is the word;" and the soil is Creative Mind. We cannot grow the flower. God blooms the rose. "Paul plants; Apollos waters; but God giveth the increase."

We must then realize that all conscious mental effort is not so much to be turned to the acquirement of things as to establish in ourselves a consciousness or mental attitude of expectancy. And no matter what process may be essential to reach this consciousness, still, in the end, this is something that we cannot do without. For consciousness is the deep-seated perception of reality! In the end, there is but one thing to do :—to believe that what we want will become manifest for us;

and then to state definitely and positively what we want.

Good exists in two forms, the good that lies within the bosom of the Father as an eternal possibility, but unmanifest and undifferentiated; and the good that we choose. Before we choose, it is a universal concept. After we choose, it is an individual concept and becomes an individual possession.

Being in the Process of Becoming.

The word is made flesh and dwells among us, only after we speak the word. So the second step will be for us to declare what we want. This is our choice. For practical purposes, I have found it especially desirable in severe cases to establish the practice of lying down immediately after luncheon or dinner or both, and then to realize the truth. At this time, spirit in the form of food, drink, and air begins to pass into physical form and energy. If one will be quiet and realize that spirit is thus passing into another manifestation, that being is becoming, and will thus impress this idea firmly upon his own consciousness, the physical body will respond to his mental equivalent and health will be the result. In cases of so-called indigestion and dyspepsia and those ailments which most readily reflect mental states, this method has secured especially quick results, for the stomach is a perfect mirror of the mind. Indigestion and colds, being due to chaotic thought and worry, are easily healed by the calm and poise of one who rests for a moment in the infinite realities of Spirit. "In quietness and confidence shall be my strength." "My health cometh from the Lord, which made heaven and earth." "Thou wilt keep him in perfect peace, whose mind is stayed on Thee." The realization of Spirit—myself as Spirit, my body, my conditions and my world—is the whole aim of metaphysical treatment. Let this once be accomplished and man stands forth, an immortal, glorified and glorious, god to his own world, at one with the infinite harmony. Life swells to its banks with the tides of a divine joy; and man rises to sit on the throne of his being. Being has in him become.

CHAPTER XIII.

USING THE LAW OF IMPERSONAL MIND IN THE CASE OF PROSPERITY.

MANY believe in the power to demonstrate over the body without being able to understand the control of circumstances, environment and prosperity. Of course, this rises out of a limited understanding of the law with which we deal. Many books have been written which have become acceptable to large numbers of ultra-orthodox people because they teach the "power of mind over the body" without admitting too wide a divinity to that mind, as if indeed it were a reflection upon God that He had endowed man with such vast power as the metaphysician claims for him. Such books assume that the creative mind in men is quite apart from the creative mind of the Infinite. This creative, subjective mind can be understood to control the physical organs which are under its immediate direction, through nerve and neurone, through cell and tissue, "by suggestion," and by the "new method" of which we have already spoken. According to this theory there are many minds,—not only many objective expressions of mind, but many subjective or impersonal minds. What, then, will these say when we affirm that there is only one such mind, and that it is not I—the individual that speaks—"it is my Father dwelling in me; He doeth the works."

This is the teaching of the Great Healer; and it is a great and glorious concept. There are not two minds; there is only one. The mistake of supposing that there are two minds has been the error of the ages. But we have seen that Spirit or Mind is one; and "beside Me there is none other." This being true, the mind which I call mine and which directs the physical activities of my body is the same Mind that rules the stars—not all of that Mind, nor yet a part of that Mind but that Mind acting in me as individual. We may get a figure of how this is, in the weather. I speak of the weather here in Los Angeles, as I look out upon nature's beauties, with the sun bursting through clouds, only to be covered again by the drifting fogs. Nature is in many moods to-day and shows her infinite varieties; but the weather in Los Angeles is not a part of the weather, nor yet is it the whole of the weather. It is just weather. My mind with its infinite capacities and varied moods is just Mind —"one with the Infinite Mind." This being true, I, as an individual, am in contact with universal Mind. We must not forget that Universal Mind or Spirit is not only present as Intelligence in all and a Life in All, but also literally is the All; and all nature is alive. Whatever activity, therefore, is displayed in mind, whether it be myself or the universal that thinks, must be felt all over, must register all over. Just as a word spoken into the air goes out and out in ever-widening vibrations, so my word or thought in mind goes out and out through all mind. And what is true or felt to be true in my mind must be true in every individualized consciousness at all times, and everywhere.

Accordingly if I wish to make a demonstration for prosperity, I must realize that "my word shall not return to me void, but it shall accomplish that which I please and it shall prosper in that whereto I sent it." My word is my thought, my desire, spoken into Creative Mind, and "according to my faith it shall be done unto me."

The Law of Spirit.

In making a demonstration for prosperity, therefore, I must realize that I am speaking into the only mind there is, and backed by the only power there is. The Law of Spirit is back of me. What is this law? It is the creative mind acting without reservation to create upon the image or idea which it has presented to itself. For in me, Spirit or Mind has started a new center of activity around which its creative forces are to work. To be sure, I, the individual conceive it, but who am I? I am an individualized center of Spirit's own consciousness. In me, seeking Its fulfillment, Spirit has begun Its work from a new level. As I think, Spirit thinks; indeed Spirit is thinking through me; and when there comes to me some lofty thought which sets me all aglow with creative feeling—and there is no higher joy than that of creative thought—I know that Spirit has found an outlet for itself through me. This is why one's greatest endeavor must be to harmonize himself with God, for when divine accord has been secured and we are in tune, Spirit can most easily make us the instruments of its advanced thinking. Who is an advanced thinker? Who is an illumined soul? The man who, by thorough preparation of his soul, has made himself an instrument through which God can easiest and oftenest manifest to the world.

MENTAL EQUIVALENTS.

Are we then to say that the best way to obtain prosperity is without business method? Certainly not. What we do say is that we can have only those things to which we can bring a mental equivalent. Have I a mind that corresponds to this position? If so, I may expect to hold it. Do I feel a capacity for this work? Then I may have it. What gives me what I want, then, is my mental equivalent, so that what I must seek, at whatever cost, is a mental correspondent, a mind that matches my desired good.

If I can get this mental equivalent, if I have the faith to see myself in possession of what I want

now, then I have provided a channel through which
Spirit can pass it into expression. From being or
thought, it will become or manifest objectively.
From an invisible universe, it will be bodied forth
into a visible; from thought to form. Then, suppose I need something now. Suppose I cannot
wait to cultivate technique. Very well, I must
simply realize that whatever comes to me comes
through the channel I provide. I provide this
channel by my thought. "According to my faith
—or confident attitude of thought—it will be done
unto me;" according to my kind of thought. So I
must work for an adequate concept. What good
thing can my faith conceive as mine to-day? I
must not worry about to-morrow. To-day I will
think the thoughts and have the faith that will set
me on the pathway of attainment. And if I need
technical skill before I can achieve success in the
special thing I want to do, I know the way will be
open to so care for my needs until I can train my
mind and hand for the further accomplishment.

Do I want a home? Then let me believe in a
home for myself. Let me see myself possessing
it. Let me expect it. Through such a channel,
Spirit passes. Do I want a position? Very well,
there are dozens of people who want just such a
worker. They and I both live in one mind. Let
me polarize myself as a center of attraction in this
mind. I establish in the one mind a communication
between the varied phases of mind—between my-

self and the employers—just as several wireless
instruments are in tune with each other so that
they can catch each other's vibrations. Then, by
the subtle ways of thought, because of my mental
attitude, I draw the position to me. Spirit acts
through the channel I have provided. I may have
the position. This is practical; and many have
secured work in just this way.

SELLING A HOUSE.

Again, suppose there is a house to be sold. You
may say to Universal Mind: "I now turn over this
house to you for I have no further use for it.
Give me its equivalent in what I can now use."
Then specify what you wish and expect it to come.
Spirit then has a channel to manifest a sale for you.

Or, you may desire money for any particular
object. In that case, specify not the amount of
money but the thing itself. Remember that Spirit
acts through the channel you provide. If you are
holding your thought up to money, for a trip, for
example, you might get the money but not the trip.

When I want money for any particular purpose,
I simply know that that purpose shall be accomplished. I know it is accomplished now in the
Divine Mind and that when the time arrives for me
to get the thing I desire, it will be there waiting
for me. And it is! Nor should we fear to ask
for what we want lest it be too much. So long as
we know that in some way we are giving an equiva-

lent to those for whom we work, or are giving a mental equivalent to Spirit, and are fulfilling its desire of acting through us, we shall find It "more ready to give than we are to receive!" For many of my patients I have taken liberties with Burrough's poem, and given them this:

> "Asleep, awake, by night or day,
> The good I seek, is seeking me;
> No wind can drive my bark astray
> Or change the tide of destiny."

Spirit is seeking to manifest itself as our good. One who has had much practice in acquiring a mental correspondent does not need much time to make a demonstration. He "knows;" and that finishes it. But we all find it necessary to go through the period when "just to know," is not so easy. We need argument. We need to see, reason, feel and understand. For this reason I often treat patients orally before holding the silent realization. This helps them to a mental attitude and often heals the sick. Indeed, many are cured by simply being told the why of things. Ignorance begets unwholesomeness; understanding restores the wholeness. Any one can get results by securing a realization in some such a manner as this:

Centering the Thought for the Realization of Prosperity.

Sit in the silence and meditate upon the fact that

all is Spirit. Even the things I see are spirit in Form. So-called "matter" is only a form of spirit. Spirit is intelligence so these things are full of intelligence. I am spirit; and one phase of spirit can have contact with another. The highest center of spirit can rule the lower. So I am ruler over these things or thought-forms. Difficulties, get out of the way! You have no real power. I take all your power away from me. (Go on in this way if you feel the need, pulling out all the roots of your wrong thinking and fear.) Now I know that all is spirit. I am glad that all is spirit and mind is everything. So now I open up my mind to receive this good (mention the desired object) that I want. I have a place for it. I have a right to it. Father, I accept it from Thy hand. Spirit of love, you can express this to me now. I am ready to receive it. I am glad for it. I give thanks for it. It is good to know that Thou, O Divine Giver, carest for me enough to give it. Yes, for me "every good and perfect gift cometh from the Father, with whom there is no variableness, neither shadow of turning." It is so good to know that Thou dost not change, that Thy law is perfect and dependable, that I can have this good (mention it) because Thou givest according to my faith. And now I know Thou hearest me always; and my faith does not waver. Out of Thy hand, my good now comes. I receive it now. I thank Thee now.

CHAPTER XIV.

SUMMARY OF LAW OF IMPERSONAL MIND.

WE can well illustrate the whole process of *being* as it is *becoming* manifest, or the passing of Spirit into form, in the principle of the stereopticon. The light represents Spirit or the Originating Source, or First Cause or Being. The slide or plate with the picture on it represents the point of transition in which the undifferentiated light begins to differentiate itself. It must be remembered that the *light is the same* whether it be at the source, the center, or the end of the series. It is light always. Spirit is spirit always; no matter what form it may assume. But just as the prism will refract the rays of the sun into the cardinal colors and cast the rainbow on our desk so the slide in the lantern will *mold and form* the light into the very form it will manifest on the screen. The slide represents our thought, idea, or image. What we choose, what we desire, what we expect, what we fear, what we believe in —these are the thoughts which mold and fashion *being* as it passes into manifestation in our lives.

THE WILL.

The lens by which the rays of light from the picture are concentrated represent the will. Using the word *will* as meaning choice, we find that we have the ability to choose what we shall hold as an image of thought. Using it as meaning concentration, we find that we have the gift of will or determination which keeps the mind "one-pointed" until all be fulfilled. The light, then, which is Creative Mind, will keep working upon the model of our thought only so long as we hold the model before it. Being infinitely creative and impersonal, it will take any idea and begin to construct accordingly; and every word we speak and every thought we think is backed up by that power. It is the purpose of the will to insist that the mind shall hold on to its desire and its purpose until spirit has passed into the desired form.

THE MANIFESTATION.

The picture on the screen corresponds to matter, body, conditions, form. It is being become manifest. It is spirit occupying space and time. "Matter is spirit at its lowest level." So while we distinctly see a real picture on the screen, still the substance of it is light or spirit. How absurd to call it illusion since it partakes of the eternal substance and will persist so long as the thought persists. And if thought is not real, then nothing is

real; and God is not real. I cannot conceive of God
without thought. What I conceive is also His conception, since we are one; and as impersonal mind
He acts for me as my creative power. So whatever I conceive will be registered on the screen,
that is, in my body and in my affairs.

WHERE FAULTS AND ERRORS LIE.

Now if the picture is faulty, what do we do?
Do we say it is not there, merely because we do not
like it? No. Do we try to rub it out? No. We
know that it is an effect produced by an antecedent
cause. So when bodies are sick, and poverty shows
its gaunt face, if we are wise we do not seek the
remedy in the effect, by beating the poor body,
pounding, or drugging it, or by rushing more madly
into the world of competition and financial struggle
to right our affairs. We are looking to the light and
"if thine eye be single, thy whole body shall be full
of light." So we center our whole thought upon
the idea with singleness of purpose.

Where, then, do we find the cause of the inhar-
monious picture? Not at the beginning of all do
we find the error. The light is all right; spirit
is one hundred per cent perfect. It is perfect *as
substance* all the way through. There is only one
other place to look and that is at the slide or
thought, where light or spirit begins its transition
into form. Here we find the error. We have a
faulty image. Our conceptual faculty has been too

low. Our pattern was imperfect. The light had
to take the medium we provided; Spirit or Creative Mind, "shining on the just and the unjust"
with equal impartiality, has passed through into
manifestation. Spirit cannot do otherwise. To refuse its light to any one is to deny to such an one
his individuality or power of self-choice, and thus
to defeat its own ends. For man is a purpose of
God; he is the object of Divine love; and in him
Love seeks its own fulfillment. So it must have the
love we *choose* to give it; or it cannot have love at
all.

CONCLUSION OF STUDY OF IMPERSONAL MIND.

We have thus studied the process of a demonstration when it is made from the standpoint of
Law acting under the impulse of our own thought.
In this method, Mind acts as the receptive and
creative agent; but our own thought gives it its
initial movement in our affairs. Our choice is all
the will it has as impersonal mind. Thus the en-
lightened soul performs a godlike act when he simply proposes to himself that his soul shall realize
the divine mind at work upon his problem, and
then chooses the pattern which it shall follow for
his health, his supply, and his happiness. When
the inspired mind of the individual reaches this
point, he has learned how to pass over to spirit all
the weight of labor. He foregoes all struggle for
he calmly voices his idea and knows that spirit not

only *will* work things out for him to the definite conclusion, but *is now* working them out. Being is becoming manifest for him.

What We Think All Day, Counts.

While we may seek moments for quiet realization of the deep things of life and for concentrated thought upon any idea, yet we are not to suppose that the attitude of mind for merely half an hour will determine the issue. It is what we think all day that counts; and we can carry on *all* the mental activity while we are about our other affairs, if we wish. Our thought must be continuously right if our manifestations are to be so. We cannot expect Being to continue to pass through our thought into expression if we choke up the channel. To choke the channel is to make another choice; and spirit will begin to work on the new idea, whether it is for our good or not.

Finally we would caution those who are always turning to the creative mind for *things* only, always impressing it for something. There is nothing wrong in the act itself, for the law is our servant; but its reckless use may lead to a sort of callousness to higher emotions and then degenerate into fakirism or worse. It may finally lead to black magic, which is the destructive use of the law. Or, with even honest minds, it may create the habit of thinking of mind as merely a delightful grab-bag from which something is to be extracted all of the time.

This is fatal to the finer instincts; and it is in order
to avoid this that we are told by no less a teacher
than the Great Master, "Seek ye first the kingdom
of God and his righteousness; and all these *things*
shall be added unto you." In other words he recognized, as we must, that creative mind is personal
as well as impersonal; and we must seek to align
ourselves with its onward movement and higher
purposes if we are to realize the perfect joy of
being. We have already considered the impersonal
nature of mind; let us in the succeeding chapters
consider it as personal.

PART II.

BEING AS THE PERSONAL SPIRIT.

CHAPTER XV.

THE GOD WHO HEARS US.

WE have all had experience of God as the Personal Spirit. There is no one of us who has not at one time or another turned his face away from everything that earth can promise or threaten, and looking up, has declared, "O God, all this is nothing if there is not something bigger than this and beyond it." Or like David, we can say in the midst of trouble, "I cried unto the Lord; and he heard me and delivered me out of all my distress." And even he who "cries out against God and dies" has a sense of God as personal, but entirely unjust, responsible for the pains he bears.

It is not so difficult to appreciate the personal nature of God as it is to prevent the mistaken idea that God acts within the limits of human personality as it is ordinarily conceived. You or I, for example, often feel ourselves impelled by circumstances to do something that we would have preferred not to do. Necessity seemed laid upon us though this really comes as the consequence of previous choices. But God acts with perfect freedom

119

though always within the law of His being—that is, His choices never embarrass Him afterwards though He Himself cannot violate His own law or even be conceived of as desiring to do so. Again we have only a limited knowledge of things so that we often make mistakes through the partialness of our knowledge. This brings unhappiness, sickness, and poverty. But God must know all intuitively and at once. Beginning and end are one with Him. Then we think of our self as distinctly different from other selves and in a sense apart from them so we hate some and love others. But God, as the Absolute Self, must include us within Himself and could not think of Himself as apart from us but only a part with us. We, as selves, have a sense of time and space. In Absolute Being, there can be no time nor space, because space denotes that which is limited, and time denotes that which is incomplete; and God is fully conscious of freedom and completeness.

What we have just said refers to God, of course, as an unique self. And by this I mean a self that is conscious of itself as a unit. If God can think of Himself as a unit, then He can think of Himself as a person. So we cannot get away from the fact if we would, and we would not if we could, that God is He who has a heart of tenderness, a mind of love, a nature of wisdom, a power that can execute His commands. He knows and loves us.

It is apparent, therefore, that while God shares

in our experience of thinking, feeling and willing, still He is never limited as we are. He knows all that is necessary to be known to answer our every problem. He loves us enough to want to answer it. He has sufficient direct contact with us to make His will effective. "He is able to do exceeding abundantly above all we ask or think," said the Great Apostle.

We must therefore insist on thinking of God in a complete way, not in a partial, for otherwise we should return to the old way of attributing to Him likes and dislikes, sometimes willing us good and at others sending us evil. Note these two facts and we shall avoid further trouble: First, GIVE TO GOD EVERY ATTRIBUTE *of personality that will not interfere with His absoluteness; purpose, thinking, willing and feeling are His*: second, *nothing in the personality of God should ever be construed as denying personal choice to the individual; He becomes even more impersonal to our will and choice than our friends do; and His purposes are so vast as to constitute law which we can depend upon as never opposing a will to our own.* Let us therefore mention the three ways in which God is personal and how His personal nature differs from our own.

GOD AS THE PERSONAL OR ABSOLUTE SELF.

The essential qualities of personality are purpose, the power to think, and the power to choose. Personality is often used to mean individuality in its

narrower sense and to convey the idea of charm
of manner or its reverse. But its true meaning
must be primarily to indicate that by which one is
constituted as a self, the persistent I, the ego that
lies back of everything I do and think. An ego is
a thinking self. God is such. He is personal in
that He can and does choose what He shall do, and
when and where and how He shall do it. He
conceived the whole scheme of the visible creation. He planned the vast system of interrelated
worlds, and the entrance of man onto the stage of
human life; He chose definite areas within the
reaches of space wherein He should set universes
to evolving, and suns to light the farthest reaches
of time. He started these suns on their ageless
journey, and fed the universe with energy to sus-
tain them in their courses.

It is quite impossible to have an effective impersonal mind without the personal, whether it be
in the case of God or of man, as we have already
seen. For we saw that it is of the nature of the
impersonal mind to act only on the ideas given to
it. Once give the idea or thought to this mind;
and it will take the suggestion and go on creating
indefinitely. So persistent is its activity that we
may count on it from age to age and call it law.
Such a law we perceive in the very movement of
the planetary bodies of which we have just spoken.
There is the law of the attraction of gravitation,
of centrifugal and centripetal force. These and

other laws seem to be in the eternal order or purpose; but they sprang out of the personal choice of Being ‚at the beginning of time, since Creative or Impersonal Mind can act only on the idea first presented to it. In order to set its impersonal creative forces to work, therefore, Spirit had *first* to choose the ideas and things It wanted made. In so choosing, It was personal. Thus It is the Personal Choosing Self that presents these ideas and to that extent God is personal.

It is for this reason that we speak of the Absolute Being as He. Of course, the term is not designed to indicate gender but only Person. We simply put into words an idea through the best medium we have and speak of God as He. Our inner concept of father is not that of gender, but only of protecting love, and so we speak of God as our Father. "Our Father which art in heaven." "Your Heavenly Father knoweth what things ye have need of before ye ask them." "It is my Father's good pleasure to give you the kingdom." He is "the Father of mercies and the God of all comfort." These are the words of inspired seers who felt this personal nature of God and were conscious of the Divine Presence.

Yet right here we must 'ware the mistake of the ages in endowing God with those impossible personal attributes which have made of Him a human idol. So much vaster is His personal self and nature than our own that to us all His acts are by the law of His being. He has set forces into operation which are as impersonal as the forces of our own subliminal self. These are under our control so far as we have the understanding to use them. These forces of life, love, wisdom, truth, beauty, supply, and so on, are God acting as impersonal mind; and our self, acting as personal, can use them even as God's self, acting as personal, can use them. Moreover, God will never interfere with our use of them. We may choose wrongly, and be hurt; we may indeed destroy ourselves physically with our choice.

In this, God will not interfere. We need never fear that His will is opposed to our own. In our personal affairs, God does not will at all. He places the law at our disposal and becomes our wisdom if we ask it. He will not force His wisdom upon us. If a man ask bread, he will get bread; if he ask fish he will get fish; if he ask for a stone, he will get a stone. In other words, the personal nature of God cannot be construed into any concept of God which interferes with our personal freedom and choice. And this the student should carefully note. Otherwise he will have a fickle deity, not because God is fickle but because He becomes to us a response to our thought. If we think that things come by the chance good-luck of His favor; then that is our law; if on the other hand we believe that He is not personal at all, then the universe presents to us a hard and pitiless mechanical machine. Let us recognize in God, then, the power of self-direction and initiation in the larger affairs of His splendid plan without thinking of Him as having, with respect to ourselves, purposes contrary to our own. In the matter of choice and love even God must not interfere, otherwise we are His puppets and unworthy of His love, and our love for Him is a hollow dream. He might as well love a stone.

THE PERSONALNESS OF GOD.

We shall find, in the second place, that in God are the diffused qualities of personality from which our own individual ones are drawn. We could not derive them if they were not inherently in Him, just as one could not draw salt from the sea unless it were there in solution. There is no thought that has ever come to man that did not once lie within the undifferentiated substance of the eternally possible. Every word we utter, every invention we make, every statue we carve, must lie as potential thought or idea within the Infinite Mind. So you and I could not have the personal qualities which we have unless they first lie latent in the Divine and Perfect Life. Whatever qualities we may have of personality, must have welled up from the Infinite Personal Life. Hearing, seeing, smelling, tasting, sense of touch, thinking, feeling, willing, loving, imagining, are possessions of the personal life; but they emerge from Him since He is all.

So what Troward calls the "personalness of Spirit" constitutes the personal nature of Him from whom all things proceed.

GOD INDIVIDUALIZED AS PERSON.

But it is through us that God becomes most distinctly personal. He puts these qualities of His "personalness" into each of us, or rather He becomes each of us, while at the same time retaining His powers and attributes. God rises to the highest self-expression in us. It is for this reason that any one of us might rather wish to be what we are —God in the individual—rather than to be God in the universal sense. For in our objective, personal self, God has ventured on His greatest quest. He is having the fun of choice in the individual unfoldment of life with all its unknown factors and its possible allurements.

We are therefore distinctly *purposes* of Being. For it is of the very essence of personality to purpose, to initiate and to select; and one does not start anything nor choose it without relation to a plan. Spirit, therefore, has purposes which it designs to work out both *for* and *in* the individual. This reveals Spirit as acting in just the opposite character of the Impersonal Mind of which we have said so much. In that, we found Being acting as the *receptive and creative agent*. In this, we find it as the *active* agent.

THE PURPOSE OF SPIRIT.

To deny that Spirit has purpose and intention of
its own is to lose contact with It at Its highest and
most delightful level, for to deny this is to remove
all sense of relationship to that purpose and thus
to cut ourselves off from receiving its benefit. The
purpose of Spirit is to express—from ex and primo,
to press out—the Life, Love and Wisdom which It
feels within Itself. The whole end and aim of
creation is manifestation. This is the ultimate.
And the individual personality, you and I, play
our part in Spirit's self-expression. We are not
apart from, but a part of, Its unfoldment. This
beautiful truth reveals man as playing a high rôle
in Love's fulfillment. Ancient is the saying, "God
made the world for his own enjoyment." If so,
man is not so much designed to use Spirit as to
be used of Spirit. Spirit would enjoy Itself in us;
and we must learn our part in this great scheme.

THE MOTIVE, LOVE.

We must first of all, then, perceive Spirit's purpose, if we are to work with It. It can have but
one, self-expression; but it may take many modes
of activity. And back of it all must be one supreme impulse, love. The bosom friend of the
Master says, "Every one that loveth is begotten
of God. He that loveth not, knoweth not God,

for God is love. . . . No man hath beheld God at any time: if we love one another, God abideth in us; and His love is perfected in us: hereby we know that we abide in Him and He in us because He hath given us of His Spirit." The presence of love then is a token of the indwelling of the Spirit; and in the expression of this Spirit, we link ourselves into the great creative purpose, and become one with the Infinite Life. We lose all sense of separation, and merging ourselves in the ocean of the perfect Life, Love and Supply, we pass from death to life, from the cottage to the palace of the King. It is infinitely worth while then to study Spirit from the standpoint of Its purpose and motive.

CHAPTER XVI.

THE GOD WHO LOVES US.

SPIRIT'S motive, we say, is love. What is love? Love is the union of two kindred things. It is that completeness which comes from this union. I care not where you look, you will find life incomplete without such a union. The whole visible universe is but the outer manifestation of this inner principle. It is shown in the chemical affinity of the atoms. Without this drawing together of kindred things, all material substances would fly apart and pass into chaos and incompleteness. In the vegetable world, we perceive the presence of this principle. The seed-bearing plant cannot give birth to another plant until the female flower is fecundated by the male. Long before sex organs were discovered in the plants, the ancients, as in Egypt, recognized the separate sexes of the plant. Heroditus says the Babylonians knew it and suspended male clusters of dates taken from the deserts over the female dates to fecundate them.

One does not need to illustrate further. All nature proves the presence of the principle of love,

or the union of two kindred things to form a real
completeness. We must see then that Originating
Spirit shares the nature of Its Creation. It, too,
must be Love, for there cannot be an expression
without an expresser, no love without a lover. God
is love.

Spirit therefore seeks Its own completeness by
passing Itself out into individual expression in man
whose first nature is love and then finding Its own
completeness in enjoying that love. The motive
of creation is Spirit's self-realization in love.

Spirit has, consequently, a further purpose,—to
continuously evolve a higher and still higher individual upon which it can pour out fuller and
ever fuller measures of Its love and life. For
Spirit is infinite in its potential; and, having once
started, it carries on to the nth degree. To learn
how to swing into harmony with this divine purpose is the end and aim of all true teaching. For
once we are in the current, It of Itself will bear us
on Its bosom to those islands of the blest where
Love and Life await us and where we may spend
our days in the never-ending joy of the complete
life and the divine companionship. "And I saw a
new heaven and a new earth: for the first heaven
and the first earth are passed away; and the sea is
no more. And I saw the holy city, new Jerusalem,
coming down out of heaven from God, made ready
as a bride adorned for her husband. And I heard
a great voice out of the throne, saying, Behold, the

tabernacle of God is with men, and He shall dwell with them, and be their God; and He shall wipe away every tear from their eyes: and death shall be no more: neither shall there be mourning, nor crying, nor pain, any more: the first things are passed away."

This is a perfect picture of that state in which man finds himself when he is identified with the purpose of Spirit. Love has found in him its fulfillment; and life has found its completeness. We can escape unhappiness, pain, and poverty, in no way so easily as this—the identification of our purpose with that of the divine. We do not have to struggle nor to make anything. We only have to be something—at one with the Infinite Spirit.

Wouldst thou find pardon for all thy transgression—
Peace from thy battles and strife?
Make thou the Peace of the Lord thy possession,
Make thy self one with His life.
More life, more life,
Ye who shall seek it shall find
More love, more love,
One with the Infinite Mind.

MAKING OUR UNITY.

The question then arises, "If all our good comes from this unity with life, how is the union to be accomplished?" And the answer is, you do not have to accomplish it; you only have to recognize it. It already Is. Separation is only apparent. It never really was anyway. You have nowhere to go outside of the Infinite Mind. There is no outside. You only thought you were outside.

At the same time, the Divine Life and Love has no reality for you until you recognize it. "Behold I stand at the door and knock. If any man will open, I will come in." You are the gate-keeper; and your door will never be forced. The Father comes out to meet the returning prodigal; but He does not drive him in. In reality, the Son never got out of the Father's love. He only thought himself out; and all he had to do was to think himself in. He thus came to himself.

Our object then is to find our own completeness in love, and to give Spirit its completeness in our love. We are to recognize Spirit as love, and turn our love-side to it, not merely our mind-side.

When this has been done, we shall also find the great secret of healing power. For if Love, Life, and Beauty are the symbols of completeness, then their opposite is incompleteness or the lack of these qualities, or fear, death, ignorance, want, and pain. Then to heal disease it is not necessary to tinker with the effect which is due to a lack of something, but to supply the deficiency. Disease is due to a negative factor; and we heal it by supplying the positive factor—love. This is the principle a man would act upon if he had an empty reservoir. He would not talk about its emptiness, complain about its stagnant odor, nor bewail its unsightliness. He would simply open up the channel to the heights and let the water flow in. How simple the process —"Let" or allow the water to flow in! The empty pool is filled without effort. The effect is changed by the cause. How well the Great Teacher understood this! "On the last day, the great day of the feast, Jesus stood and cried, saying, 'If any man thirst, let him come unto me and drink. He that believeth in me, as the scripture hath said, from within him shall flow rivers of living water.' But this spake he of the Spirit which they that believed in him were to receive." He is speaking of the great inner self when he says "me," for we are expressly told that he spoke of it in relation to the Spirit. So we have a further picture of the glory of man's nature and the healing process. If any man will open the pipes at the bottom of the pool, the water or the Spirit will fill it like a spring.

The word "Spirit" as it occurs in the Greek text is "psyche" which also means "life." If, then, we are to be rid of death and disease and "lack," we have only to let Life flow in from the inner springs of our being. And the touchstone to Divine Life is Love.

I breathe the life and love of God,
  The spirit-raptured air,
And feel the thrilling, vibrant force
  Of Him whose ardent care
    Enfills the whole:
I breathe His life as one who quaffs

From out the sacred cup,
Who drinks the wine of God, the Vine;
For, as he turns it up,
God fills the bowl.

I thrill anew with health and peace,
While through my veins asurge
There flow the full-breathed tides of health
That cleanse, inspire, and purge
From pain and strife:
I breathe more deep the pranic air,
Drink deeper still the bowl;
For as I drink, from Life's full brink,
God fills my thirsty soul
With His own life.[1]

_____

[1] *Songs of the Silence,* by the author.

CHAPTER XVII.

THE GOD WHO HEALS US.

LOVE therefore is the great healing power. It is its absence that causes incompleteness or disease. It is its presence that causes health or wholeness. Love is completeness or wholeness. And such completeness or wholeness is necessary for both the soul and the body. He who can administer the great palliative of love to the broken-spirited serves mankind whether he succeeds in restoring the body or not. A friend of mine, a trained nurse, tells me of a case to which she was called. The physician stated that there was no possibility of recovery and the nurse was therefore to make the last days as comfortable as possible. The woman was in the prime of life; and in her bitterness at pain and death, she had turned even against her own family with a sort of hate. The nurse, being thoroughly acquainted with the principles of mental science, said nothing at first except in a nurse's capacity, but began at once to declare the presence of love. She stated silently, "You are full of love; and only love is around you." This continued for several days at the end of which

time the woman said, "Nurse, you are good to me.
I love you." Shortly after she said, "I am so full
of love. It seems that I love everybody." Then
she and the nurse had talks together; and she said,
"I know I am not going to get well. But I feel
that I am healed. Do you think that anybody could
feel that way if they were going to die?" "Yes, I
know you are all right," was the reply. The woman died declaring her faith and love.

Now some one may think that this is not a good
example of the healing power of love; and yet what
was it that the woman needed first of all? She
needed the restoration of a sense of wholeness, of
unity. That is love. And she needed that for
whatever plane of existence upon which she might
live. Her very self seemed restored to her. There
is no question that she would have been healed if
the case had been taken before the idea of incompleteness had taken such a hold on the impersonal
mind that the contrary idea of health did not succeed in supplanting it.

Cases have come to my attention or experience
in which the thought of love has caught up those
who otherwise would have passed on, and restored
them to the love and service of their families. One
of our healers was called to such a case in which
the woman had been given up by the physician to
die of tuberculosis. "She has only four days to
live," said he. With a divine compassion of self-
giving which I have seldom seen equaled, the healer

called her back from the edge of the grave; and
at least two years later than the time of which I
speak, I knew of her as carrying on the housework
in her own home.

Feeling and Emotions.

Let us consider the reason why love plays such
a divine rôle in the cure of souls and bodies.

We all understand that love is "feeling." The
first nature of Spirit is feeling; and Its motive is
to express this feeling so that we often speak of
First Cause as Original Feeling. The creative
power is therefore emotional. We find the same
thing true in the individual. The subjective faculties govern all the unconscious activities of the body,
causing the heart to beat, the lungs to expand, taking in the life-giving air, building the new cells of
the various organs and expelling impurities. These
subjective faculties are emotional. The seat of
the emotions is not objective; our objective faculties have only memories of emotional experiences.
Feeling and emotion are subjective and creative.
It is a well-known fact that it is not the "holding
of a thought" that heals; it is the feeling that ac-
companies the thought. How often we have noted
the physical change accompanying strong feeling.
An angry man grows red in the face. A fright-
ened one turns white. His hair stands on end, his
flesh creeps. Brave men tell us that this happens
even in the case of those whose will still drives

them bravely forward. One of Napoleon's staff said to him of a certain officer, "Did you see how pale he turned when you gave him his orders?" "Yes," replied Napoleon, "but he will nevertheless do his duty."

Colossal hidden energies reveal themselves under the stress of strong emotion. Many cases have been cited in which some crippled person has risen from his bed and accomplished prodigious deeds, as in cases of fire where the need was imperative.

On the constructive plane, the same process occurs both in the individual and universal creation. An idea is taken into the mind. The strong emotional creative forces play upon it and build on the model; and our greatest ideal passes out of thought into real expression. It is thus through feeling that the ideal becomes the real. It is through love that the word becomes flesh and dwells among us. This was the understanding of the poet who wrote:

"One thing shines clear in our heart's sweet reason,
One light that over the chasm runs,
That to turn from love is the world's one treason,
And treads down all the suns."

THE CREATIVE FACULTY, LOVE.

Right here is where so many fail of results. They get the right thought but not the feeling. They have an intellectual persuasion but not an emotional. They do not feel its truth. No song sings itself in the heart. No pulse beats warmer. No surge of joy breaks on the shore. Not that one must lose intellectual balance, for there is nothing unnatural about feeling; feeling is normal and divine.

But we do not need to "work up" love from somewhere. The heart that goes out in natural expression to find completeness in another or in the Originating Feeling Itself, goes because it rejoices to go, gives because it is glad to give. It does not calculate on return. It is not seeking something; it is simply being its true self. The great loving, compassionate heart of the Master Healer drew men unto him, and made him the great healer that he was. He did not love men in order to heal them: he healed them because he loved them. Healing was not an aim but an inevitable result. Healing is a by-product of consciousness. The illumined mind heals because in expressing love it also acts creatively. The creative faculty, therefore, is love or feeling. The greatest healers to-day are those who, out of a great love for folks, are willing and eager to help them untangle all the snarls of life, and say to the troubled waters of their souls, "Peace, be still." Disinterested affection is divine. Self-giving is godlike.

> "I built a chimney for a comrade old,
> I did the service without hope of hire,
> And wandered on through winter's cold
> Yet all the day *I* rest before the fire."

We thus see that love finds its own completeness
in self-giving. The Master Teacher further illustrated this principle by saying, "He who would save
his life shall lose it; but he who will lose his life
for my sake [for the sake of love] the same shall
find it." Love is complete only in expression, never
in holding it back. Life is fully realized only as
we love. One can see this so often illustrated in
great-hearted men and women who have applied
this truth. Love being the finest and most harmonious of all vibrations has worked a very miracle
of change in the fine molecular structure of the
flesh. Radiant health flushes to the overflowing
banks of life. The smile of such a person is a
blessing; and his laugh a delightful contagion.

This then is the result of true feeling; it is an
end, not an aim. Love has its own rewards in
love. Love is worth while for its own sake.
"Love is the fulfillment of the law." It is fulfillment or completeness without which life falls into
elemental chaos. So Spirit seeks Its own completeness in making its union with that other self within
it. The question, therefore, is the one already
asked—how can we coöperate in the work of Spirit?
The answer we shall find in the next chapter.

CHAPTER XVIII.

THE MYSTIC UNION, OR HOW TO REALIZE THE PRESENCE.

L IFE finds its completeness only when the full purpose of Spirit is accomplished through us. It seeks an object worthy of its affections. Being passes out of the Absolute into the individual and becomes you and me that it may find such an object. For outside itself, it would be impossible to find it, since God is all. Man is therefore born for love. Human life can never be complete without the union of the individual consciousness with the universal. The final search of the soul must therefore be for this wholeness of being. It is this wholeness that we are all after, whether we express it in one term or another. Even he who seeks for things, instinctively recognizes that they follow *after* the consciousness of unity; they never precede it. We must harmonize with Spirit before It can work effectively through us. But in addition to the general consciousness of the Divine Unity, there is the craving of every natural man for a personal sense of relationship with God. The quest is a personal one. As the mystics have said, "It is the flight of the alone to the Alone."

To coöperate with Spirit in fulfilling its design of ever higher self-expression, it becomes necessary for us to move toward It as well as It to move toward us. Love on our part can mean nothing unless it is spontaneous. Spirit cannot force us to love. It cannot force us to coöperate. In the mechanical creation, everything can be made to be obedient to law. To man alone is given the power to disobey. To him alone belongs this high power of deliberate choice. He can give or withhold. To be sure he himself is incomplete so long as he withholds, with an incompleteness or unwholesomeness that results in limitation, sickness and death.

Man holds therefore a glorious freedom, to choose his own pathway. And it is when he *voluntarily* surrenders his heart in loving union with the Spirit that he gives It a unique pleasure. In this sense, man himself becomes necessary to Spirit's own enjoyment. So while man may stand aloof; yet if he does so, he must suffer from incompleteness, which, being the reverse of completeness or good, is evil. On the contrary, if he chooses to find unity with Spirit, he will find with it that peace, poise, and contentment which rises out of his wholesomeness. And this which comes to him comes not as the end to be sought but as universal plus which is added by creative mind to our reward—"seek ye first the kingdom—and, all these things shall be added."

It must be, therefore, the spontaneous activity of the heart seeking its own completeness in self-giving—in the loss of self to find it in the Greater Self.

Through the Silence to the Center.

We must realize, first of all, that we are in the quest of wholeness. Everything that we see and most that we experience is related to something else. Everything is an exhibit of parts. We are to strive to enter into a feeling of the essence from which all this multiplicity proceeds. We are after an at-one-ment with the Absolute. This can never be secured objectively, but only within where the relationships of things find their relator. We must pass by the portals of sense, beyond thought into feeling. The mystic consciousness "may be gotten by love, but by thought, never." It is in the realm of the intuitions that we find the More-than-Self, the Proofless Proof of life. Here is the Light Eternal. Once a skeptic friend came to the great spiritual leader, Debendranath Tagore, the father of the poet, and said, "You talk of God, ever and again of God! What proof is there that there is a God at all?" Tagore pointed to a light and asked his friend, "Do you know what that is?" "Light, of course." "How do you know that there is a light there?"   "I see it; it needs no proof; it is self-evident."   "So is the existence of God.   I see Him within and without me, in everything and through everything; and it needs no proof: it is self-evident."

In the silence, one is not after proofs, but only after that which to the soul will be self-evident, a vision of the All, and, finally, *union with the All.* And, as the very climax of life is reached when we can on the one hand express in the world of the relative, and on the other, be conscious of the wholeness of the self, let us not be disturbed if it takes time fully to realize ourselves in either direction.   We must find our place in both worlds, the outer and the inner.   At the same time, most of us get so tangled up in the world of effects that it. takes effort to move into the world of cause.

Concentration and Meditation.

The first step,[1] therefore, to the mystic consciousness, is concentration.   We must bring the mind to one point of interest and keep it there.   Our purpose is to center the mind exclusively on the desired object, the recognition and realization of the Divine Presence.   To this end, we may, if we wish, make statements leading in this direction.   "I affirm the oneness of Being and my unity with the All." "The Father and I are one."   "I am entering into

---

[1] The five steps mentioned here are similar to Miss Underwood's analysis of the mystic's consciousness.   See *Mysticism.*

the secret place of the Most High where I may abide under the shadow of the Almighty." "I know and believe in the love which God hath in me. God is love; and he that abideth in love, abideth in God and God abideth in him." "There is no fear in love: but perfect love casteth out fear, because fear hath punishment; and he that feareth is not made perfect in love." "We love because He first loved us." "I am not alone, but I and the Father that sent me." "If I know myself, I know the Father also. From henceforth, I know him and have seen him." "The Father loves me." "Father, I have glorified thy name and will glorify it." "Thou, the Spirit of Truth art now come, and dost guide me into all truth; and Thou dost declare Thyself unto me." "O righteous Father, I know thee, because thou art my Greater Self revealed."

One-Pointedness.

Let me say here that these and similar statements which we all will make as expressing our determination to know God and to realize Him are not to be made merely at some stated time; nor are we to seek this realization for the moment only. We must continuously practice the idea of a Real and Vital Presence. We find this wonderfully accomplished in the life of Brother Lawrence, the Medieval Saint. He claimed that "the practice of the presence of God is the greatest rule for a holy life." His wandering thoughts were again and again brought back to the one-pointed desire to realize the presence.

It is this fixity of purpose or mono-ideaism that strongly impresses itself upon the field of the inner consciousness where there is complete realization of the connection between the self and God. Unity with the Absolute can be had only by determined desire and the continuous subjection of the mind to this one idea, "that I may know Him." Gradually we shall be enabled to withdraw from consciousness of the relative, more and more into the quiet state of mind in which the Voice can speak to us. By maintaining this attitude of expectancy, the mind is at length brought to a certain poised calm which the mystic has called the "quiet of the soul."

THE QUIET OF THE SOUL.

By a proper effort of will, the mind can be brought into a quiescent state wherein the busy call of earth is stilled; and the noise and clatter of sense is forgotten.

> The wild throbbing pulse of my spirit
> So troubled with earth's din and strife
> Is stilled in the presence of stillness;
> Serene in this temple-like place,
> A peace seems to press all around me
> And hold me in loving embrace.

Having reached this delightful solitude of the soul, many mistake it for the ultimate, and there rest in the untroubled sea of silence. They are

however still only in a mental state. Yet some believe themselves to be already "in the silence,"
and seek to do the work of healing on this plane.
But the great healing power is not found here.
Nor is the true mystic after quiescence; he is after
realization. So he passes through the antechamber
into the temple.

Actual Perception of Being.

The stillness is but the atmosphere in which Spirit
speaks to us, for it is impossible to "hear the voice
of gentle stillness," when the sense-life is making
its call upon our attention. The heart can now become entirely absorbed in the joyful perception of
God and real communion with the Absolute. We
feel Him not as a part but as a Whole. The
Psalms reflect this feeling. Take for example the
Sixty-third Psalm of David.

"O God, thou art my God, earnestly will I seek thee:
My soul thirsteth for thee, my flesh longeth for thee
In a dry and weary land where no water is.
So have I looked upon thee in the sanctuary,
To see thy power and thy glory,
Because thy loving kindness is better than life;
My life shall praise thee.
So will I bless thee while I live:
I will lift up my hands in thy name.
My soul shall be blessed as with rich living;
And my mouth shall praise thee with joyful lips,
When I remember thee upon my couch
And meditate on thee in the night watches."

"When I meditate on thee in the night watches," —this is contemplation. How expressive this sen‑ tence! The music is stilled; the harpist has dozed away into forgetfulness; and all the palace lies asleep, save the king who "meditates in the night watches." What are his meditations? To each is given his vision. But each in his own way per‑ ceives the Presence, beholds the Infinite Whole. Emotion runs scale after scale on the chords of being. Some pass into ecstasies, some have visions, some like Saint Theresa and Saint Katharine of Siena swoon into ecstatic sleep, to wake to won‑ der and to power of service.

But we are not to suppose that the phenomenal experience is necessary to the full enjoyment of God. It is indeed a delight to feel the full joy of the Divine Companionship sweep over us; and this experience can become the possession of all. Every‑ where is God; and we may abide in Him. One can‑ not be lonely, for there is no place apart from Him. We do not carry the burden alone for He will help us to bear it. Sorrow can be but for the moment, for within is the everlasting joy seeking to burst out and flood the soul. Fear must step from the pathway, for in God is our divine protection; and no evil can come to the heart that trusts in Him. "Fear not, for I have redeemed thee; I have called thee by thy name; thou art mine. When thou passest through the waters, I will be with thee; and through the rivers, they shall not overflow thee:

when thou walkest through the fire, thou shalt not
be burned, neither shall the flame kindle upon thee.
For I am Jehovah, thy God, the Holy One of Israel,
Thy Saviour." On every hand is the All-Good; and
He is there holding limitless resources in His hand.
"His arm is not shortened that it cannot save."
All else may fail; but God cannot fail. The sky
may darken, but within the shadow still we may
feel the guiding hand. Friends may desert us; but
"when my father and mother forsake me, then
the Lord will take me up." Plans may go wrong,
but the Divine and perfect pattern still remains.
The thread may tangle for a moment in the warp
or woof of life; but the final fabric will still be
woven; and we shall receive each his wage for the
work he has done. Life is endless; and what fails
in one place must yet succeed in another. For
my part, I am sure that there can be no ultimate
failure, for whatever the heart may crave exists
perfect somewhere; and we shall succeed in every
venture. We dare to trust to the long vision and
believe in the final outcome of all, because we are
in union with the Perfect Life and move on to perfect ends. In our becoming, in our self-expression,
we may at times work with faulty hands; but the
Master Architect will find a place for each man's
work; and the Ultimate of Being in us will at length
express its perfection.

And for us the reward is sure for it is the reward
of love.

"And only the Master shall praise them,
  And only the Master shall blame;
And no one shall work for money,
  And no one shall work for fame:
But each for the joy of the working,
  And each in his separate star,
Shall draw the thing as he sees it
  For the God of things as they are."

Thus all labor is a labor of love, and receives the due recognition—the immaculate approval of one's own soul, and the blessing of him whose eye notes every sparrow that glides through the silent blue.

But in the mystic contemplation of God, the mind is not filled either with the thought of evil or of good, of fear or of faith. It is filled only with the exquisite consciousness of the Presence. The consciousness represented by this experience which we call perception or contemplation usually remains with one as the satisfying ultimate, the goal of the soul, for a long period of time. It seems joy enough to know and feel the Presence of the All. Yet this is not the ultimate of the possible experience; and in time there is a craving for a more vital one. We desire not only to *know* All or see All; we desire *unity* with the All.

CHAPTER XIX

THE MYSTIC UNION—THE SOUL'S DARK HOUR—THE LIGHT ETERNAL.

IT is usually at this point in our experience that we have the dark hours; for in letting go of that which has heretofore filled our lives in order to grasp a greater reality, we seem often to lose our grip on all and to go flying far in endless space. I think this is quite a common experience of those of nobler sort who are passing out of the old order of religious thought into the new. They have had a real and vital experience with God. They have "known Him in whom they have believed;" they have through intensity of interest reached the stage of a true contemplation of God; and it is for that very reason that they have launched out into the deep. It is at this point that they come into the fellowship of the New Order seeking higher experience. But whether they are in the old order or the new, the period of transition is often very painful. Of necessity, the concept of God must be entirely changed, often enlarged; and we become space-wanderers. Some I have seen who have apparently lost themselves in the very

vastness of Truth. The concept of a manlike God
has been discarded. The new understanding of
the personal nature of God is not yet made clear.
One is lost on a psychic sea. One is dazed by the
effort to take bearings in the wide vistas of the impersonal mind. Prayer is frequently given up, because one does not pray to Law: one orders it,
one does not entreat it. In former days, we begged
favors of God and *hoped* that He would grant
them. Now we see that we get what we want by
expecting it enough! We choose what we want;
we believe in it; we take it. Where does God come
in? He seems rather a supernumerary in this new
order until we suddenly discover that *it is not things
we want, but God.* Or if it is God that we have
wanted right along, we at length find that He can
be had for the asking.

> "Bubbles we earn with a whole soul's tasking,
> 'Tis heaven alone that is given away,
> 'Tis only God can be had for the asking."

Most of us have had this experience in one form
or another. We have lost our one-time joy, and
have passed into the shadow. "Why," we ask, "do
I pass into this depression? I have seen the
heavens open. I have been on the sunlit sum-
mits. Now I move in darkness; and I cannot see."
Sometimes the worse appears the better reason:
"The things I would, I do not; the things I would
not, those I do; and there is no health in me." Life

runs to counter currents; and one moves out of error into mistakes.

Well, this is the dark hour of the soul, indeed; but it must pass. And in the darkness we hear a voice, "Lo, I am with you alway even unto the end of the earth." And again, "Heaven and earth shall pass away; but my word shall never pass away." "I will send the Comforter unto you. He shall teach you all things and guide you in the way of truth." These dark experiences of the soul may be short-cut by the use of the Law for it gives back to us in form what we give to it in idea, and manifests according to our demand. Boldly declare therefore, "The Law of Life and Mind makes for me just what I demand. Let the true understanding of God be revealed to me. Let life put me on the path of truth." And the last great surge of the sea shall cast your frail bark on the golden sands of God!

A TREATMENT IN THE "DARK HOUR."

To help you to realize this vision and this union, I have prepared the following statement of Truth: I abide in the conscious Presence of Spirit. I am enclosed in the life of the Infinite. I am encircled by the Ever-loving, Ever-living Joy of Being. I draw upon the limitless resources of God. I am sustained and strengthened by eternal forces. The love of my Father presses in on me on every hand. I stand on the Rock of Ages. The strength of the hills is His also; and it is mine. Thou Ever-Present One, Thou art my life and my supply. I rejoice in Thee for there is fullness of joy where Thou art. I cannot for one moment be outside Thy presence and Thy care. Thou art always everywhere; and there is no place where Thou art not. I cannot be forgotten in Thy mind; I cannot be lost from Thy consciousness, for Thou art the One and only Mind in which all things and thoughts exist. I cannot be separated from Thee for Thou art the Whole and there are no parts without nor within. I will no longer think of myself as lost nor estranged from Thee. I will not believe that Thou art angry with me, or condemning me. Thou art loving me. Even though my father and mother forsake me, Thou wilt take me up.

For Thou art love. I abide in thy love. I rest in it. I breathe its air; I feel its warmth. I know its joy.

"From love to light, O wonderful the way
    That leads from darkness to the perfect day:
From darkness and from sorrow of the night
    To morning that comes singing o'er the sea.
From love to light. From light, O God, to Thee,
    Who art the Love of loves, the eternal Light of light!"

Then fear not the darkness, for if thine eye be single, thy whole body shall at length be full of light. Thou shalt find the Rock of Ages and stand on it.

THE UNION COMPLETED, OR THE "UNIFIED LIFE."

The onrush of the soul at last brings it into the final harbor—"the unified life," the "deified life," where we can say, "I and the Father are One." Here the experience is quite different from that in "meditation." There we only meditated upon God as All; here we find ourselves, not as one without, *looking on,* beholding some one apart from us, but as one *within,* merged in the Divine Life. Nor is it a sentiment, a pretty figure of speech. It is not a philosophic statement of being; it is spiritual realization or feeling of Ultimate Reality.

This, then, is the very goal toward which we have been struggling—the feeling of Ultimate Reality. We have been trying to make our union with It. Returning thus to our query, "How can we cooperate in the work of Spirit," we reply, "By making our union with it in divine self-giving." It seeks completeness in love, for love is the union of two kindred things; but It cannot find this completeness without our coöperation. "God is Spirit; and they that worship him, must worship him in spirit and in truth, for such the Father seeketh, to be his worshipers." He does not force. Here God must stand and wait. We must unbar our own door.

BEING.

To come into this consciousness of at-one-ment

with Spirit is to come into the realization of being.
Life cannot be complete until we realize ourselves
as being and enjoy it. This is not the Being of
God—the "Greater I Am;" nor my being—the
"lesser I Am;" but it is the realization of myself in
God. The Greater I Am is Absolute or Undifferentiated Being without individual realization.
The lesser I Am is the individual without recognition of its absolute relationship. The developed
consciousness is the realization of the self in Spirit
so that we can say as the Great Teacher said, "All
power is given unto me."

BECOMING.

We thus reproduce in ourselves a new center of
intensified consciousness, really a new starting point
for spirit in its own self-expression. We must
never lose sight of the fact that Spirit through us
is seeking self-expression, and has high purposes if
we will coöperate. We have no higher purposes
for ourselves than It has for us and through us.
Coöperating with It, we have Its infinite power,
wisdom, and love to work with.

We must remember, too, that Spirit is seeking
self-expression through manifestation. Spirit is
always passing out of being into becoming. If we
are its highest point of departure for new manifestations, then being will become or manifest through
us into its highest form, *if we will allow it.*

CHAPTER XX.

INTUITION, OR THE HIGHER WISDOM OF THE UNIFIED LIFE.

SPIRIT is seeking through us its own self-expression. To be in harmony with Its purposes, is to assure the success of our own; for what we want It wants for us. I suppose that the full significance of this cannot be fully appreciated by any of us at first. But it means no less than that Spirit will pass through us into health of body, wisdom in affairs, plenty in possessions, happiness, and a true greatness.

How then are we to keep in harmony with Its purposes? Retaining firm grasp on the fact that Its purposes are general while ours are specific, we must realize that what we are after is some way by which we keep from making the mistaken choices which lead inevitably to disaster and inharmony. And this way is provided in the very fabric of the law which we have been studying. If we do not know the right choice to make, Spirit, as the infinite Wisdom, will help us to make it. If we do not know the form which it should assume, Spirit *does* know. "The Father knoweth what things ye have need of before ye ask them."

Here we pass into direct consideration of Spirit from the opposite standpoint of the use of the law, from that in which we made choices and presented them to impersonal mind to create for us. In that phase of Spirit, It is receptive, passive and creative; and *we* direct its forces. In this, we find Spirit as the active, formative, sending agent. The former we have illustrated by the use of the stereopticon. This we can best illustrate on the principle of the camera.

ILLUSTRATION OF USE OF INTUITIVE.

The mind of the individual who is seeking guidance or impression of idea from the Guiding Wisdom is represented by the film, which is free as possible from all impressions and is seeking such. The lens represents the concentration of the mind upon this one idea or purpose,—to receive guidance. The shutter represents an act or choice by which we open up the mind to receive definite suggestions, and which is open only to such points of the landscape as we wish to have impressed upon the film. For even here we exercise choice, that is, we choose along what line we shall have guidance. The landscape represents the formation of the idea into definite form in the idea plane, that is, the Divine Mind. The light is Spirit, Wisdom, Power. Through it alone direction comes. It is the substance and the source of all. Light is Being passing into form or becoming manifest.

This is the use of the intuitional faculties. We are quiet that we may be instructed. To be sure, we establish the image of desire; but it is simply that Spirit shall give us wisdom and direction along a given line. We do not wish to dictate; we wish merely to know.

So if you see no way out of your present difficulties, know that there is a way, and that Spirit as Wisdom knows that way. Or if you do not know *how* a thing should be done, nor how it should appear, yet Spirit as the Creative Mind or Formative Wisdom does know. All form emerges from it.

Escaping the Lash of Experience.

It is the work of the intuitions to find out for us just what is the best thing to be done, or to be chosen. It is thus that we are kept from the grievous errors and pains of wrong thinking, and bad choices.[1]

We do not desire to be always in the chains of our mistakes, or to be ever learning through bitter experience. If we must learn all there is to know only by blindly stumbling forward, and through bitter hardship and suffering acquire life's lessons, we are doomed to a life of hell, for the possible combinations of experiences are endless. To say, then, that life is merely a quest of experiences and that

[1]See pages 172-178 in "Intuition and Ideation" in *The Law of Mind in Action,* by the author.

we are here to learn through them, *is to say that the purpose of living is to learn what not to do. This is as false as the Devil.* Life is eternal; and, if we are to know only by the experience of broken law how to avoid error, then the goblins will get us in the form of Karma.

But we must realize that all knowledge already is. What we are to do is to learn how to use it and to bring it out into objective manifestation. Thus do we find help in the knowledge of the personal nature of Spirit, for as It already contains within Itself all possible and potential form, It will select for us the form most desirable, if we will advise with it.

INTUITIVE KNOWLEDGE IN HEALING.

In the case of healing, all we have to do, then, is to give Spirit an opportunity and to realize that it is now passing through into manifestation along a given line. Let us take, for example, the treatment for tuberculosis. The lung has been manifesting partialness of idea or unwholesomeness. What we wish to do is to make it manifest wholesomeness. Having taken an easy position so that you are at perfect rest, place your hand on the body just over the lung and say, "Spirit is now passing through into expression as a perfect lung. 'The word is made flesh and dwells among us.' I know that there is within me the spirit of wisdom that knows just how to form you into the perfect organ, and

it is so forming you now. The mind in me that
formed you in the first place, reforms and restores
you now according to its own perfect pattern."
One will naturally go on in a similar vein until a
great consciousness of healing rises up within
him.

This method is not dissimilar to the so-called
"new method" of the psychologist who talks to the
cell-life and encourages it.   That is, however, direct
"suggestion," conveying the impression that we
must "do" something, while this seeks merely to
awaken the consciousness to the fact that something is being done for us, but which would not
be done unless we called the healing agent into
activity. We are simply to realize the active presence of spirit. We do not know how a lung looks,
but *it*, as the formative power, *does* know.

What we must seek is a definite feeling of wholeness, and after some practice we shall find that
we do feel the life forces at work for us. This
feeling will in turn react upon the thought to give
more faith and courage.

Now what has really happened? In the first
place, we must recognize that we are dealing with
Mind and that as there is no element of time or
space in Mind, as such, it manifests with all Its
Power and presence wherever it is recognized.
Neither psychology nor physiology will teach us
differently. We know where the brain is located,
but not the mind. Again, even though thought oc-

casions movement in the brain cell, not all of "mind" is there. We therefore center mind as active by realizing it as present in any part of the body. Then, as active, it must work on its own creative life model. As Professor James has told us, "All mental states are followed by bodily activity of some sort." This is what we are after, to feel the presence of Mind. Thus our mental attitude will be followed by corresponding activity first on the emotional plane and then on the physical. We do not get out of the body to heal it, but rather perceive Spirit as directly active in it. There is no need to deny the body. On the other hand, we are not dealing with the body apart from Spirit—"apart from me, the spiritual self, ye can do nothing"— but rather with the body as spirit.

Identity with Spirit.

What really occurs is that we recognize spirit as such. We identify our body, our conditions, and ourselves with Spirit. THIS IS THE MARRIAGE OF BEING AND BECOMING. This, then, is the important thing, to get a realization of Spirit, whatever method you may follow. I have secured good results with patients who have used this method; but I would not recommend touching any part of the body that is sore or swollen. In that case, I would recommend only the thought of Spirit as active there—Spirit as the Perfect Life working out its own pattern of lofty perfection.

I have thus illustrated the principle of the use
of the intuitive powers in the way of image-forma-
tion. From the standpoint of guidance in affairs,
and such things, I have dealt with intuition in *The
Law of Mind in Action;* and the reader who is inter-
ested can turn to those pages for help. Here our
object is rather to see how completely our mind is
at one with the Cosmic on every plane, and how
readily we may identify our life with the great impersonal mind, and our purpose with the forward
movement of Spirit. It is in this perfect harmony
and understanding that our future peace and happiness rest.

There are a thousand ways to speak but only
one language—thought; there are a thousand cen-
ters of individual consciousness—but only one
Source—Divine Mind; there are a thousand forms
but only one Power—Spirit! "Ask, and ye shall
receive; seek, and ye shall find; knock, and it shall
be opened unto you." And for him who would
rise in the scale of being, who would intensify
Spirit's center of consciousness in him, what exercise more replete with meaning and delight than
simply to count over the sweet promises and the
loving certainties of life, to dwell on the joy of
real living, to dream over the wonders of a world
all spirit, to see God in stars and sunsets, to listen
to wee wild things; and then in the silence of the
soul to "be still and know that I am God."

The proof of God lies not in nature or authority,

or revelation; it lies in the quiet of man's soul, when in infinite peace and calm he rests upon surpassing love and is satisfied. "Thou wilt keep him in perfect peace whose mind is stayed in Thee."

CHAPTER XXI.

DOES DEATH END THE PROCESS BY WHICH BEING BECOMES?

BECOMING is the process by which either God or man expresses being. With God, there are evidences of eternal unfoldment and self-manifestation. Is it so with man? For him, is death inevitable? Is immortality assured? Our answer to these questions must be based on the law of personal and impersonal mind. While it is possible that revelations have come to us from those who have passed through the portals of what we call death, nevertheless if we are to depend upon these for *proof* of immortality, the majority of mankind would have to rest without conviction, because in the nature of the case, only a few could come into such vital touch with the spirit world as to get the proof. Such at least is the present status in the study of psychic phenomena. It is probable that it will be many years at least before the average person can have these proofs presented to him personally, if at all, and even then he must struggle with the problem as to whether the voice he hears

comes from "Beyond," or only out of his own subjective mind or by the creation of his odic forces.

Yet, within this science, lie all the proofs that
are necessary for the highest conviction and faith.
Let us review the facts. If I can know anything
at all, I can know I am. If I can know I am, I
can know that I think. If I can know I think, I
can depend upon the sanity or reasonableness of my
thinking. My observation and reason show me that
I live in a living universe, visible and invisible, and
that this universe is made of Mind and by Mind.
I can also perceive evidences both of a personal and
an impersonal activity. The personal activity is
the choice of what shall be made. The impersonal
activity is the creation of the thing that has been
chosen. These facts I find true not only of the
universal mind but also of my own. I also find
that since the universal mind is by its nature *one*,
whatever thinking *I* do is done *within* the one mind.
Then, since the impersonal mind must create in
form and substance whatever is given to it as a pattern, it must create on the pattern *I* give to it.

The Idea of Immortality Impresses Its Necessity on Creative Mind.

What pattern do I inevitably give it regarding
my own immortality? Is there any idea of which
I am more certain than my determination to live
forever? Is not the first law of life, the preservation of the self? How often we have heard it:

"Self-preservation is the first law of nature." Do
I not continuously think of myself as an individual
entity in the Cosmic Mind?   There are, to be sure,
those who are like the New York schoolman who
said, "I do not want to live forever; but I believe
I shall."   But this is after all because the burden
of life has become so intolerable that some would
escape from it altogether.   But after all the cry
of such souls is for freedom.   They dread life because they are bound.   Even the suicide is not so
much trying to escape life as he is making his pro-
test against being limited.   He believes that he will
secure more life by leaving this one.   That he must
pay the penalty of his rash act goes without saying; but that he illustrates the primal instinct of
human life, is also clear.   All, all demand life, freedom, *self*-expression.   The survival of the self is
imperative.   I have never known any one who
would be willing to exchange his self with any
other.   He may have a desire for another's cul-
ture, education, wealth, opportunity, and so on, but
never that other's self.   He feels instinctively that
his self is all right; but it must have an opportunity.

The idea of immortality is found in every race,
every age, every individual who has risen to any
height of moral attainment.   And that idea is thus
persistently held in the cosmic, creative, impersonal
mind, which must construct according to the idea
given to it.   Life is a creative fluid and makes anything and everything given it to make.   It throws

all its resources around every idea and will continue to create around it so long as we hold the idea within the depth of the sea. If, then, the idea of individual identity is forever instinctively held in mind, it will forever hold us as individual within the bosom of its greater self. We are immortals. No Greek or Roman god ever topped the earth with such colossal, inherent, and glorious power as moves and beats within the mind and heart of each of us. To what glorious immortality we are destined by the very faith within us, which no hardship, no limitation of ignorance or despair can ever down, the immortal faith in the immortality of the self. Said that great Master Teacher who understood these principles so well, speaking to Martha of the physical death of her brother, Lazarus, "I [the ego-self] am the resurrection and the life; he that believeth on me, though he die, yet shall he live; and whosoever liveth and believeth on me, shall never die."

All of us instinctively believe in the ego-self, and therefore all shall live forever in individual freedom of the self. Said Jesus again of those who are reputed dead, "But as touching the resurrection of the dead, have ye not read that which was spoken unto you by God, saying, I am the God of Abraham and the God of Isaac, and the God of Jacob. God is not the God of the dead but of the living." Thus unto God all are alive;

and the instinct of immortality is the instinct of God Himself in our own soul.

What that further life holds for us we shall not inquire in detail here. One or two things we may note from the law. It is foolish to suppose that through death we change the entire thought-content of the mind, that bad men are made perfect, and the pious at once enter into the felicities of eternal indolence. The margin between the best of us and a perfect life would be so great as to constitute a total loss of identity if the chasm were to be crossed at a leap. The continuity of experience demands that we go on in even development "over there." Thus there will be all grades of society and of interest. Again, as we draw around us those who most fit the thoughts and ideas of our own mind, we shall have society over there that is most like ourselves. We shall have our friends and probably our enemies. We shall each have his own work to perform. But the beautiful thing about it is that we shall all go on in unfoldment and that there can be no doubt that the very desires of our heart will draw to us those whom we love and who love us.

DEATH.

Is death inevitable? Must all die in order to live again? Turning once again to the law of impersonal mind we see that it manifests to us just what we give to it in idea. What then do all of us give as an idea of life and death? We give the race-idea, of course. It is the experience of the ages that we repeat. Man has said, "Whatever is mortal dies. Man is mortal. Therefore man dies." This was the logic which the sense-experience gave and to which the sense-experience has assented. And so death has visited the race from the beginning of time to the present. Moreover we live in a world wherein form is in constant change and transition, and is a part of the order of the visible creation. Man is therefore impregnated with this idea from birth. Can it be changed?

Whether the idea of physical death can be changed, depends upon what we mean by it. If we mean the idea of pain and wracked physical senses in the transition of life from one plane to another, I can say that the idea *is* changing. Death is no longer looked upon with horror, nor is the struggle severe with advanced souls.

If, however, we mean that man will eventually live forever on this plane, I do not believe it. I think it absurd to debate it. We are changeless beings in a world of change. This plane can never hold for us all the possibilities of self-expression which is the purpose of life. We must go on. But perhaps we shall learn how to transmute the body without allowing it to pass through the ordinary stages of dissolution. The body itself is unconscious life or mind, that is, thought which is vibration and has been organized as a form in which to house the soul. Some of the lofty ones of earth like Elijah, Enoch, and Jesus seem to have known how to pass the unconscious life-substance back into elemental form and to have taken on a spiritual body without leaving the physical one in form. Whether we shall all reach that point of power, I do not know. One thing is certain, that in either case the body is entirely changed; and I cannot see that it matters much whether we leave it in the air as oxygen, hydrogen, and various elements, or whether we leave it in the ground. In either case, it is the death of the form and not of the soul.

The change in form is therefore inevitable and desirable for the on-pushing soul in the quest of great adventures. Nevertheless it should not be painful; and, in the majority of cases, death itself is easy; and the pains that attend it, whether mental or physical, are as nothing compared to those experienced by the same persons in the course of the disease which takes them away. Death, then, may come to the human frame, but only with great peace and sweetness; and in days to come we shall see preparations made accordingly, and instead of the palpitating fear and agonized desire to keep the reluctant soul one day more on earth at no matter what cost of painful medications, we shall see the beautiful passing of the spirit into other fields of love and self-expression. Thus the death-bed will become the scene not of a taking-off but a taking-on; and, in place of thinking of our beloved as passing into the final act of dissolution, we shall think of them as now taking the primal step in the re-birth of the soul. Before our very eyes, the beautiful *beginnings* of life are being effected. Says Paul, "Now this I say, brethren, that flesh and blood cannot inherit the kingdom of God: . . . then shall come to pass the saying that is written, Death is swallowed up in victory. O grave, where is thy victory? O death, where is thy sting?"

CHAPTER XXII.

"I AM HE."

WE have discovered then that there are definite areas of the unseen with which man is to-day becoming familiar, even though he has learned them only by carefully feeling his way through the darkness of the ages. By a thousand tests, by experience, by revelation, by reason, by his very hopes, he has forced something of the unknown to reveal itself to him; and his accumulation of facts has been sufficient to enable him to plot a law of life and to lay the basis of a new science, new to him, but to the Eternal Mind known alike throughout the past, the present, and the future, which to God are one. What, briefly, is this science? Its facts are these: We live in the midst of a vast sea of cosmic intelligence which manifests in everything that crystallizes, everything that sends forth a bud, everything that builds a cell, everything that thinks a thought. It is formless and thus constitutes the substance of form: it is being and thus is the basis of all becoming: it is impersonal and thus assures the only possible foundation for the personal in us or in itself. It is homogeneous, can never be separated into parts, and thus embraces all within its own being. It is infinite intelligence, for all that we know or think emerges from it; and it declares itself on every hand. All that intelligence does, it does; from it emerges every faculty we possess. It displays purpose for it chooses by more than chance. It is law and yet above the law: it is law, because it moves relentlessly from cause to effect and never, so far as we know, breaks the rules of its own mighty game: it is above the law, for law is merely the way it works. Its choices are cosmic; and, in our affairs, its will is ours; it has none of its own that contradicts ours. It is force because the unit of energy is everywhere the same,—thought or vibration. As one, then, it is the source of all that we can know or do or feel. It is thus wisdom, life, love, beauty, supply, and hope, and all. Having no will opposed to our own, it becomes to us just what we look for. As Mind it acts by thought, and therefore we control our own destiny by applying to it through the medium of our thinking.

Above all, it is love, for love is the essence of unity, and being *one,* it must live in eternal harmony, so that whatever exists within it can adjust to it without friction, and by the same token can adjust perfectly to all other manifestations of life and mind. Its supreme nature is love, for this is the quality of life that underruns all other qualities, things and expressions. In this is the final hope and the eternal peace of man, for love can never deny itself, and as the object of an eternal and supreme affection, man stands at the apex of the spheres, king not by power nor by might but crowned by the chaplet of Divine Love.

Spirit as All.

Thus, in the ultimate, we come to the one great need of human thought, the distinct necessity of recognizing Spirit as *All*, from Alpha to Omega. It is *being* passing into expression in *becoming*, just as the light of the stereopticon is the same from one end to the other. And our age demands a realization of this one fact above all else—that Spirit is all, in all, and through all.

God is Spirit or Life, and in Him we live, move, and have our being. And we must learn to make our identity with Him. Not to lose identity in Him, which is Nirvana, not to be less ourself but more ourself, this is what we seek. We are points of intensified consciousness and expression in Spirit. We are Being manifested in becoming; but being and becoming in the ultimate are one. The need of this age therefore is not merely a message but also a messenger; let the messenger be the message. We need not so much the teaching of truth as its manifestation in human form. We must see the Word bodied forth in flesh. This is the secret of Jesus, "Glorify thy Son, that Thy Son may glorify Thee: even as Thou gavest him authority over all

flesh . . . And this is life eternal that they should
Know Thee, the only true God, and him whom thou
didst send, even Jesus Christ. I glorified thee on
the earth, having accomplished the work thou hast
given me to do. And now, Father, glorify Thou me
with the glory I had with Thee before the world
was. I manifested thy name." Jesus thus identified his being with that of the Eternal Creative
Spirit; and he rightfully claimed that in his person
this Spirit was manifested. In him being had its
perfect becoming.

"I AM HE."

Our age demands the same glorious manifestation of the sons of God. Of us, Jesus himself tes-
tified, "I say ye are gods." The only God that
men shall ever see is the God in and through men
and a manifested creation. "This is the secret hidden from the foundation of the world, Christ in
you, the hope of glory." Each of us in greater or
lesser degree is a manifestation of Spirit; and I
do not wonder Peter could exclaim in the presence
of Jesus, "My Lord and my God." I, too, looking
into the face of a godlike man or woman and seeing in such an one God manifest, could exclaim
without shame, to the God within and manifest,
"My Lord and my God."

We hear many voices to-day declaring the way to
truth and life. Let us follow our teaching by embodying it.

"For none of the singers ever yet
Has wholly lived his minstrelsy,

Or lived and sung that life and song.
Might each express the other's all,
Careless if art or life were long,
Since both were one to stand or fall.

So that the wonder struck the crowd,
Who shouted it about the land,
His song was only living aloud,
His work a singing with his hand.

Let or allow the new Messianic figure to appear
in you. "Some great cause, God's new Messiah!"
The cause is that of God's own divine self-expression in humanity; let us be the expression. When
we speak, let men say of us, "I believe that man,
for he is one hundred per cent expression on every
plane—spirit, mind, and body. He Is what he talks
about." Jesus was, and exclaimed, "I am he."
Let the new Messiah also appear exclaiming, "I
am he." "I am" is the absolute of being. "I am
he" is the process of becoming. Then when being
and becoming have found perfect union, the mystic
marriage has taken place; and God has accomplished Himself in us. Already there are men and
women on the planet who have found the divine
union; and the day dawns when they shall step
forth saying, "I am he that should come." And
the way for this to be universally realized is to

recognize that "it is not I that speak, but the Father dwelling in me, He doeth the works." Thus to recognize that which already Is, is to cause it to be so manifested. *Being and becoming are then one.*

THE END.